everyday
discipleship
for
ordinary
people

STUART ◆

BRISCOE

EVERYDAY DISCIPLESHIP FOR ORDINARY PEOPLE

VICTOR BOOKS®

A DIVISION OF SCRIPTURE PRESS PUBLICATIONS INC.
USA CANADA ENGLAND

Recommended Dewey Decimal Classification: 248.5

Suggested Subject Heading: CHRISTIAN LIFE—DISCIPLESHIP

Library of Congress Catalog Card Number: 88-60203

ISBN: 0-89693-565-5

To
Dave and Debbie,
Greg and Judy,
Pete and Libby,
family, friends,
and real disciples all

contents

Ordinary People Make Extraordinary Disciples

SHE HAD BRIGHT RED HAIR and blue eyes. Sitting cross-legged on the floor in the middle of the room she was surrounded by the rest of the group sitting stiffly in chairs arranged around the perimeter. Some sat with arms crossed over their chests as if to protect themselves from whatever dangers might be lurking in the meeting about to begin. Others had their hands folded neatly on Bibles which rested primly on their laps, implying by their body language, "I'm here to be good. Please don't do anything to make it hard for me." And all of them had carefully averted their eyes from me, hoping to avoid being asked the first question. When I say "all of them" I except, of course, the "bright one" sitting on the floor. She was raring to go and her open face and eager look all but shouted, "Come on, man. Let's get this show on the road!"

The show in question was the inaugural meeting of a group of men and women who had indicated interest in becoming members of our church, and who were about to embark on a three-month "pre-membership class."

I needed an ice-breaker, so turning to this one obviously anxious to participate I asked, "Would you mind telling us your name, please?"

"Sure. Nancy," she replied.

"And tell us what you do."

"I'm a disciple of Jesus Christ very skillfully disguised as a machine operator," she responded without a moment's hesitation.

Nancy's response certainly provided the ice-breaker I was looking for, but it provided much more. Even as the others laughed at the way she responded, they realized Nancy had not only made a personal statement but had presented a challenge to everyone in the room. The laughter soon subsided and in its place a sense of introspection and evaluation settled on the group. We all began to think how we would have answered the question, "And what do you do?" and I suspect that few of us would have answered as she did.

Of course, the most common way to answer this frequent question is to state an occupation. "Oh, I sell insurance." Or, "Well, I guess I'm just a housewife." But to see oneself as first and foremost a disciple of Jesus Christ is refreshingly different.

We don't use the term *disciple* much anymore, preferring rather to talk about being a *Christian*, a term which unfortunately is so full of ambiguities and misunderstanding that it has become almost meaningless in modern parlance. Then again, if we do talk about discipleship, it is usually in the context of a course we are taking or a structured approach to Christian living which requires specific amounts of carefully monitored exercises carried out under the supervision of a "discipler." We convey consciously or unconsciously the impression that to be "discipled" is to be part of a spiritual elite. "Oh, did you know that I've been discipled by Rev. So-and-so?" Or, "I'm almost through with my discipleship study and now I have to find someone else to disciple."

But to see one's discipleship as something lived out on a factory floor amid the noise and clamor of machines and the hustle bustle of labor-management relations is appropriate and encouraging and not at all common.

My red-haired friend reminded me anew that disciples are ordinary people so living their lives in everyday circumstances that the touch of Christ is evident to all who care to watch. Their experience of Jesus Christ is such that the mundane surroundings in which they live and move have the glow of heaven upon them, and the dull boring tasks which of necessity they must undertake become invested with divine significance. So real and powerful is their relationship to Him that He influences their responses to secular pressures and governs their reactions to human actions. These very ordinary people live very extraordinary lives.

Yes, the redhead reminded me that ordinary folks make wonderful disciples.   ♦

Christians Were Called Disciples First

THE CHAPTER TITLE DOESN'T LOOK quite right, does it? That is because it is almost a quote but not quite. Acts 11:26 reads, "The disciples were first called Christians at Antioch." But I stated it this way for a good reason. While the expression *Christian* is much more popular today than *disciple*, the Scriptures talk much more about disciples than Christians.

Moreover, long before the term *Christian* was invented (probably as an uncomplimentary nickname), those to whom the name was given were known as *disciples*. A good case can therefore be made for using *disciple* rather than *Christian* because Christians were called disciples first.

So what? Well, I wouldn't want to build a doctrine on it or start a denomination but I think that because the word *Christian* is used so much that it means so little, it might be a good idea if we gave *disciple* another look. Let me illustrate.

Airplanes are wonderful for getting from A to B provided you don't mind visiting C and D and have your baggage deposited in X, Y, and Z. Airplanes are also great for good uninterrupted reading time unless of course you sit next to Mr. Talkative. Because of the kind of books that I read on long flights and because I seem to attract the Mr. Talkatives of this world in much the same way that lighted candles attract moths, I am often asked the following question:

"Are you a Christian?"

"Yes," I reply, smiling warmly in a befitting manner, but not warmly enough to encourage the conversation. "Yes, I'm glad to say that I am."

"What kind?"

"I beg your pardon?" [Spoken with a slightly exaggerated British accent.]

"Are you a born-again Christian or one of those liberals?"

"Oh, I see what you mean. Yes, I'm a born-again Christian."

"When?"

"Pardon?"

"I asked when you were born again? If you're born again, you'll know when you were born again."

Sensing that reading time is lost for this leg of the flight, I put down my book and try to explain that Billy Graham knows when he was born again—responding to the preaching of an old Southern evangelist named Mordecai Ham; but his wife Ruth—who was born of Presbyterian missionary parents in China—cannot name the day nor the hour when she first believed. "But as Billy says, 'If Ruth isn't a Christian, neither am I.'"

By this time I know that I am suspect, and further questions are forthcoming.

"Are you a Spirit-filled, born-again Christian?"

"Do you mean Spirit-filled in the charismatic sense or Spirit-filled as understood by the Reformed segment of the church?"

"I mean are you Spirit-filled?"

"Yes, I can honestly say that I seek to live under the lordship of Christ, in the power of His Spirit, rejoicing in the enabling that He gives for every demand He makes upon me, and confident that He will continue to gift me appropriately for the ministry that He has given to me."

"Well, what about the Millennium?"

"What about it?"

"Are you a premillennialist?"

"Well, let me put it to you this way. The more I study the Millennium, the more I can understand the positions of both the premillennialists and the amillennialists, although I do have more difficulty with the postmillennial view. So right now I think I would prefer to keep my options open and call myself a panmillennialist."

"A what? Panmillennialist? What's that?"

"Well, I was being slightly facetious, but when you consider the millennial options which godly people have advocated—whether 'A,' 'Pre,' or 'Post'—I am undecided. But it will all pan out in the end. It was just a joke and not a very good one!" I sense Mr. Talkative does not approve of humor.

"Are you pretrib?" he next inquires.

Round about this point in the conversation I decide that as we are engaged in something akin to an interrogation to determine my Christian credentials, it is time to change the direction of the conversation. So I say, "Have you noticed how many questions you have asked in response to my simple testimony that I am a Christian? In effect, you want to know if I am

a born-again,
Spirit-filled,
charismatic or Reformed,
premillennial,
pretribulational
Christian, and we haven't mentioned denominations,
sacraments,
church government,
political involvement,
social issues, or
the role of women.
If we aren't careful, we may have to find out if I am
a born-again,
Spirit-filled,
charismatic or Reformed,
premillennial,
pretribulational,
Protestant or Catholic,
sacramental,
politically involved,
socially active,
independent or denominational,
congregational or elder-led,

egalitarian or hierarchical
Christian.

"Now, as I have some degree of apprehension about this adjectival Christianity, and as we are about to land, let me simplify everything by asking you just one question: 'Are you a disciple of Jesus Christ?' "

The response to that question has usually been most significant. Some people look blankly back at me, suggesting that they have never considered the possibility; even more disconcertingly, some say, "Well, I wouldn't exactly claim to be a disciple. I'm just an ordinary born-again Christian." This suggests to me some degree of confusion about what it means to be a disciple. Those who suggest that they wouldn't claim to be disciples but are confident they are just ordinary Christians have failed to recognize that there is really no justification for differentiating between the two.

A false perception exists that Christianity is rather like a Boeing 747, where you get on board and travel either tourist or first class. Both classes arrive at their destination at more or less the same time (first class arrives fractionally ahead but also crashes fractionally ahead in the event of an accident). If you want to make the trip as an ordinary Christian, you go into the tourist cabin; but if you are a little more particular and committed, you travel first class as a disciple. Discipleship has become a kind of optional extra for those who are so inclined, while being an ordinary Christian without all the extra baggage of discipleship has become acceptable and palatable to many.

This convenient dichotomy is unacceptable because it is unbiblical, but I must admit that I understand how the distinction came to be. While from a biblical perspective it is impossible to draw any distinction between the terms *Christian* and *disciple*, we must recognize that the word *Christian* has become almost totally devalued in common usage.

In first-century Antioch being called a Christian meant that you had been identified as one who had "believed and turned to the Lord" (Acts 11:21) and who had determined "to remain true to the Lord with all [your] heart" (v. 23). But between the first and twentieth centuries some strange things happened to

the word *Christian.* Depending on who was using the term, it
could mean anything from a religious preference ("Of course
I'm a Christian. I'm not a Buddhist, am I?") to a designation
held with scant regard by those who had a church affiliation,
without it hindering them in any way as far as their lives were
concerned. Vance Havner, the famed Southern preacher, used
to say, "I understand about homiletics. I just don't never let
them interfere with my preaching." In much the same way it
is possible to be a "Christian" in today's terms but "never let
it interfere with your living." This is barren nominalism of the
worst kind.

In an effort to counter this abuse of the word *Christian*
and all that it had stood for historically, the term *born again*
came into vogue. Here at last was a means of differentiating
between those who bear the name so casually that they prove
conclusively that "that which is lightly held is easily
dropped," and those earnest souls who have a genuine desire
to be part of the historical movement which began with the
first disciples and will be concluded only at the final establishment of the King in His eternal kingdom.

Unfortunately, something equally awful happened to "born
again." There is no question that the term is thoroughly biblical because Jesus said, "Unless a man is born again, he cannot see the kingdom of God" (John 3:3). But do you
remember what happened in the Presidential campaign of
1976? Jimmy Carter emerged from his Georgian obscurity and
announced first of all that he was running for President and
secondly that he had been born again. The national response
to the first statement was "Jimmy Who?" and to the second,
"Born what?" Mr. Carter explained what he meant and soon
the term was so popular that just about everybody and his
uncle became born again.

While there is no doubt in my mind that President Carter
did the church in America a great service by highlighting
what it means to be born again and as a result leading many
people to inquire further, it is also true that the term quickly
degenerated into nothing more than a smirky sort of expression used to describe anything or anybody that was starting
over. Football players who had arthroscopic knee surgery

were born-again athletes; businessmen who went broke, filed for bankruptcy, and started another business were born-again businessmen; and alcoholics who dried out became born-again alcoholics. Soon thereafter "born-again Christians" were forced to go back to their adjectival drawing board and "Spirit-filled, born-again Christian" hit the headlines.

Sad to say, some of the most visible and vocal of the "Spirit-filled, born-again Christians" began to do things that many self-respecting agnostics would not dream of doing; and in their efforts to separate the sheep from the goats, genuine believers looked for more terms to use as a means of putting distance between themselves and those whom they suspected of being less than true to Christ. So adjectival Christianity began to flourish, but in the flourishing began to lose its way. In the buildup of words needed to support the faltering significance of *Christian*, the simple, profound, and challenging word *disciple* slipped through the cracks.

It should be noted, however, that perhaps some believers were not sad to see the word *disciple* go the way of other ancient words like *sacrifice*, *holiness*, and *separation*. For in an era when "laissez faire" not only applied to economics and sexual behavior but also to a Christianity committed more to feeling good than doing good, and to enjoying rather than to enduring, *disciple* sounded suspiciously like *discipline*. In fact, the word even conjured up vague recollections of a book called *The Cost of Discipleship*, written by that serious German Lutheran, Dietrich Bonhoeffer, who got himself killed for his faith. Shudders!

Whether *disciple* has been forgotten or forsaken, I contend we need to breathe some fresh air into what the word really means, so that we can produce more disciples of Jesus Christ skillfully disguised as you-name-it.   ◆

What in the World Does Disciple Mean?

WHEN MY RED-HEADED FRIEND described herself to our pre-membership class as a disciple, she was reasonably assured of being understood. But if she had used the term on-the-job when talking to her fellow machinists, she would probably have seen their eyes glaze over. "What in the world is a disciple?" they likely would have asked, looking at her as if she had just crawled out from under a rock.

Well, what is a disciple?

In the first century, everybody knew what a disciple was because they were a dime a dozen. Lots of people were disciples of someone or other. And there is the clue as to the word's original meaning. Disciples were individuals who had attached themselves to somebody else, not for the fun of it, but in order that they might learn from the other person. The person so attached was called *mathetes* and the person to whom he or she was attached was called *didaskalos*, meaning "disciple" and "teacher" respectively.

John the Baptist had his group of disciples who were so committed to him that even after they had followed Jesus at John's suggestion they still retained deep affection for and attachment to him. Even when John languished in Herod's prison, they still visited him there, presumably not without some degree of risk. Such was their devotion.

The Greeks developed a teacher-disciple format for their

educational endeavors. For example, when one of their sharp-eyed philosophers noticed a hen crossing the road, he observed that before it could get all the way across it had to traverse half the road. Further observation proved what he had suspected all along—namely, that the hen's progress was accomplished by traversing such infinitesimal segments of the road that the hen was not even moving. This led to the astounding discovery that motion is made up of nonmotion. Having digested this stupendous piece of information, he then set about disseminating it for the good of mankind. And how did he do it? By the simple expedient of gathering around him disciples to whom he imparted the knowledge, with the understanding that they would apply it to their own lives (how, I know not!) and share it with others. This was the essence of their discipleship.

Not to be outdone, the Pharisees had their teachers and disciples. This was necessary because they were so zealously committed to the Law and its correct observance that they raised innumerable questions which someone had to answer. That was the job of the teachers. For example, Pharisees knew that to work on the Sabbath was to desecrate something specifically instituted by God. That was clear enough, but what was not clear was, "What exactly is work?" Carrying a burden, they decided, was work, but then some poor soul who wore false teeth worried whether wearing them on the Sabbath was equivalent to carrying a burden and therefore sinful. We might smile, but we have to give the Pharisees an "A" for effort.

What did the teachers decide? They pondered the problem and decreed that false teeth were not suitable Sabbath attire! Having determined this interpretation of the Law, it was necessary for the leaders to spread the word. And how did they do it? Through the teacher-disciple method. Pity the poor disciples of the Pharisees because they had no less than 365 prohibitions and 250 commandments to memorize and teach!

Given this environment, it is easy to see why Jesus of Nazareth chose the same method. It is significant that as soon as He embarked on His public ministry, He began to collect the disciples who would form the nucleus of His church. Mark tells us that He "called to Him those He wanted, and they came to Him ... that they might be with Him and that He might send them out to preach, and to have authority to drive out demons" (Mark 3:13-15). It is clear that the basis of their discipleship was a relationship to Christ, described so winsomely by Mark as their being "with Him" at His request. But it is also clear that the outworking of the relationship was one of service under His authority. Any understanding of discipleship that does not incorporate the ideas of personal relationship with Christ, commitment to serve Him, and readiness to live in the good of His authority is by definition inadequate.

We've all heard of love at first sight and some of us may have experienced it. My wife and I don't claim love at first sight, but we think it was probably close to love at second look. Granted, relationships can be started with a glance or a look, or a bolt from the blue, or even a collision in a corridor, but we know that relationships that matter take time and involve process. This is certainly true for healthy marriages, robust families, successful businesses, and winning teams. And it is no less true of the disciple-teacher relationship.

We need to reiterate this fact because some brands of contemporary evangelism leave people with the unfortunate impression that if they come to Jesus, He will take over their lives so efficiently and effectively that they are guaranteed to become "healthy, wealthy, and (if they wish) wise." This kind of Gospel presentation serves to make people an offer they can't refuse, but it leaves many with little idea that they are embarking on a relationship of devotion, commitment, and service to authority that will last literally from here to eternity. It is not too difficult to get people to respond to a message that promises to "meet their needs" without showing the significance of the relationship which makes the "need meeting" possible. But it can be extremely difficult getting those who have been wooed by such an approach to devote themselves to the One who has called them to be with Him and to serve Him.

In all fairness, I should point out that the Mark passage I've quoted and applied refers specifically to the Twelve. The uniqueness of their relationship to Christ was such that perhaps not everything in Jesus' call to them is transferable to every modern-day disciple. But having said that, we must remember that the Lord who called them to be disciples also commissioned them to "make disciples"; and there can be little doubt that what they had learned in their experience with Him became the substance of what they shared and the model they tried to reproduce.

The *"didaskalos-mathetes"* model also provides us with another helpful insight into the meaning of *disciple.* The Greek schoolchildren did not have to sit at desks in classrooms. Instead they were deposited by their proud parents or long-suffering slaves at a grove where lemons and oranges and olives grew. In the shade of these lovely aromatic trees stood the teacher clad in a long white robe and matching beard. Once the pupils (a.k.a. disciples) were assembled, he would start walking among the trees, sharing with them the lesson for the hour. The pupils would follow their teacher as he walked; and no doubt, being kids, they would begin to imitate his every gesture, impediment, or idiosyncrasy. In the process of time they would learn something despite themselves, and what they learned would show up in behaviors both conscious and unconscious.

Accordingly to the Greek mind, discipleship meant following, learning, and imitating. All three concepts are strikingly evident in the impact that Christ had on His disciples and are equally powerful in shaping the modern-day disciple. We will explore these concepts further in later chapters, but for now let us make sure we know how to answer the question, "What in the world does *disciple* mean?" A disciple is a person who has an ongoing, life-changing relationship with a significant other person (in this case, Jesus Christ); and who then gladly shares what he or she has learned with others.

The *Milwaukee Magazine* recently interviewed physicians in the Milwaukee metropolitan area, asking them which specialists they would go to if they or their loved ones needed medical assistance. The editors stipulated the criteria by which they wanted the physicians to evaluate their peers and then published the results. No less than seven of those chosen were members of our church, every one of whom is committed to the Lord Jesus and actively serving Him both in their careers and in many and varied ministries. None of them is a blue-eyed redhead and they don't operate machines on the factory floor. But in light of our definition of a disciple, it would be perfectly appropriate to describe them as "disciples of Jesus Christ skillfully disguised as physicians." ◆

First You Get Their Attention

I DRIVE ABOUT TWENTY MILES from my home to the church, along a road that passes lakes and woods and well-tended farms. The journey all in all is pleasant except for one detail: the road is festooned with billboards. Now, those signs may help someone's supply side economics, but they do nothing for the countryside's aesthetics. As I drive past, I am irritatingly aware of the billboards' presence, but I couldn't tell you what any of them say. Except one!

This particular billboard has half a car sticking out from it, giving the impression that someone driving too fast has gone right through the sign. Standing by the car and looking under its hood is a mannequin clad in a mechanic's white coat. When the breeze blows, the coat comes to life, and seemingly the man does too. I have passed the sign dozens of times. I know it is fake. But every single time I go by, it grabs my attention. On a road overpopulated with billboards, most of which are eminently forgettable, it takes something striking and dramatic to get ahead of the pack and grab the most jaded attention.

Before He could effectively call the twelve disciples to Him, Jesus had to find the hot button of their imagination and press it to trigger their interest. This He did over a period of time, through a series of events.

John records in his gospel account how Andrew was first

put on inquiry about Jesus. As John the Baptist was busy baptizing converts one day, Jesus walked by and John paused long enough to point to Him and say, "Look, the Lamb of God, who takes away the sin of the world" (John 1:29). This, of course, was an attention-getter of the first magnitude. When the same thing happened the following day, Andrew and another of John the Baptist's disciples went after Jesus, spent some time with Him, and came away so impressed that Andrew told his brother Simon, "We have found the Messiah" (v. 41). That was enough incentive for the action-oriented Simon, and the next day he arrived at Jesus' doorstep to find out for himself who this man was. Jesus had gotten his attention too.

Christ still does the same sort of thing today. A number of years ago, I received a phone call from a young college student asking if I would talk to her, and I quickly agreed.

"Don't be in such a hurry," she said. "I was in church last Sunday night and listened to you preach but, frankly, I didn't believe a word of it."

"Why, then, would you want to talk to me?"

"Because I think you know God."

I was getting more intrigued by the minute and so I asked how she came to be in church the previous Sunday evening.

"Some friends and I were out drinking when one of them suggested that we should find a church service to disrupt. Apparently your church is the only one in this area that has a Sunday evening service so we drove up to your place."

"Oh, you mean there was a group of you in church?"

"No. I was there alone because when we arrived at your front entrance I jumped out of the car and my friends—if you could call them that—slammed the door and drove off, leaving me very drunk and very visible on your doorstep."

"So what did you do?"

"What could I do? I came inside and listened."

This young woman came to my study later in the week and every week for the next year before she finally responded to the winsome and authoritative call of Christ to become a disciple. Her story was fascinating. Brought up in a strict Bible-believing home, she rejected "the idea of God" as a little girl, remembering quite distinctly the time when she chose no longer to believe. Settling into her agnosticism, she nevertheless developed a keen social conscience which led her eventually to embrace Marxism. A brilliant student, she studied philosophy and then went on to law school before becoming a public defender with particular responsibilities for young people involved in crime.

Now, of course, she is a disciple of Jesus Christ skillfully disguised as a trial attorney, but first He had to get her attention. And He did it somehow as she sat under the influence of alcohol in a church service where she didn't believe a word that was being spoken. I still don't know how He did it and neither does she, but neither of us doubts that He did!

A year elapsed in this young lady's experience from the time she was first intrigued by Christ until she became His disciple. How long it took Simon to follow a similar path we do not know, but we do know that a process was involved in the call to which he responded. And processes take time.

After the initial meeting with Jesus, Simon returned to his boats and fish. Jesus, who had moved from His hometown of Nazareth to Capernaum, the lakeside city Simon called home, began to preach throughout Galilee. And wherever He went, the crowds followed Him, which must have made the local fisherman less than enthusiastic about the commotion all these people caused.

One day the crowd was so pressing that Jesus asked His acquaintance Simon to lend Him a boat so that He could push out from the shore before the crowd pushed Him into the water. Simon was glad to oblige; and a few minutes later the Master sat safely in the boat and spoke to the people sitting on the shore. To show His appreciation, Jesus said to Simon afterward, "Put out into deep water, and let down the nets for a catch" (Luke 5:4).

But Simon declined for what he felt were very good reasons. He had fished all night and caught nothing, then had gone through the painstaking business of cleaning his nets, a chore made even more onerous because they were empty. He was not at all inclined to get those nets messed up again. Besides, if he couldn't catch fish before the sun was up there was little chance of getting them in the blaze of day. Yet as quickly as Simon voiced his objections, he agreed to Jesus' request: "But because You say so I will let down the nets" (v. 5). Simon said this not because he recognized that Jesus the carpenter was a better fisherman than he, but because during the time he had been able to observe the Master, he had been increasingly attracted to Him. Attention must always precede attraction.

Malcolm Muggeridge, the British author and critic, was for many years a very brilliant and articulate skeptic. His keen mind and scathing wit made for a formidable combination to debunk the many things that did not meet with his approval. One day on assignment for the B.B.C., he was sitting in the crypt under the Church of the Nativity in Bethlehem waiting for the streams of tourists and pilgrims to pass through so that he could film his commentary. The crypt itself is rather gloomy and unattractive, with many smoky lamps and thread-bare wall hangings. There is even a silver marker which purports to locate the exact place where the infant Jesus was cradled. I can think of no place on earth more ideally suited for a skeptic to have a heyday.

But when a group of pilgrims entered the crypt, Malcolm Muggeridge was strangely moved by what he saw. Some of them fell on their knees in prayer. Others began to sing quietly, while still others appeared to be in a state of ecstasy as they huddled in that unlikely place. The impact on Muggeridge was dramatic and started him on his own spiritual pilgrimage, and eventually to the place of becoming a disciple of Jesus Christ skillfully disguised as an internationally acclaimed author and television commentator.

It is easy to see how Simon became so attracted to Jesus because he could observe Him "up close and personal." But it takes people like Malcolm Muggeridge to remind us that those who love Him are the ones who can still effectively demonstrate the beauty of His person to a watching world.

The Word of God also displays Christ in all His attention-getting attractiveness. The scholar Erasmus, whom some called "the man who laid the egg that Luther hatched," was particularly concerned that the common people should have the Bible available to them in their own language. So he set about translating it for them despite considerable opposition from church officials, who were nervous about what ordinary people would do with the Scriptures. Erasmus in the preface to his translation stated his conviction: "These sacred words give you the very image of Christ speaking, healing, dying, rising again and make Him so present, that were He before your eyes you would not more truly see Him." Erasmus' words may contain a touch of hyperbole, but the sentiment is such that all who know the Bible will concur that in the sacred pages a picture of Christ in all His majestic beauty is presented for human wonder and response. Given the opportunity, He will get your attention.   ♦

Follow Me, Men!

ONE OF MY YOUNG colleagues was officiating at the funeral of a war veteran. The dead man's military friends wished to have a part in the service at the funeral home, so they requested the pastor to lead them down to the casket, stand with them for a solemn moment of remembrance, and then lead them out through the side door. This he proceeded to do, but unfortunately the effect was somewhat marred when he picked the wrong door. The result was that they marched with military precision into a broom closet, in full view of the mourners, and had to beat a hasty retreat covered with confusion.

This true story illustrates a cardinal rule or two. First, if you're going to lead, make sure you know where you're going. Second, if you're going to follow, make sure that you are following someone who knows what he is doing!

"Come, follow Me," Jesus said to Simon, Andrew, James, and John. And Mark tells us, "At once they left their nets and followed Him" (1:17-18). As we pointed out in chapter 4, this call did not come out of the blue. Contact had been established before this occasion. These men had experienced enough of the Master to be convinced that He was worthy of following. They had heard that He was the Lamb of God; they had become convinced that He was the Messiah; they had seen Him heal Simon's mother-in-law; they listened when He preached to the multitudes; they observed His actions.

This is not to suggest that Simon and company fully appreciated the significance of Christ's ministry, claims, or intentions. Subsequent events proved that their understanding was remarkably faulty. Nevertheless, they were confident enough that when He challenged them, "Come, follow Me"—whatever that meant—they were prepared to do it.

Luke's account of the call of the disciples is more detailed than those of the other evangelists. From him we learn about Christ teaching from the boat and Simon's willingness to go fishing again—against his better judgment—for no other reason than Jesus told him to. The results were nothing short of spectacular; the catch was so great that the nets couldn't handle the weight of the fish. Simon's partners were called alongside to help and both boats struggled to stay afloat.

It would not have been at all surprising if Simon had thrown his considerable energies into saving the situation that threatened their livelihood if not their lives. But he did no such thing. Instead, "he fell at Jesus' knees and said, 'Go away from me, Lord; I am a sinful man!'" (Luke 5:8) Since there is no record of Jesus doing any preaching on sin and repentance at that particular moment, we must assume that it was His majestic, awesome power so dramatically demonstrated that showed Simon, by way of contrast, what a weak, ineffectual, unreliable sinner he was. Jesus, of course, had no intention of going away. He was just starting. But surely He was delighted to hear Simon's words, because they showed that this headstrong fisherman was at last ready to follow. Up until that time one might wonder whether Simon was humble enough to be a follower, given his natural preference for being a leader.

When Jesus talked about marriage He insisted that there should be a "leaving" and a "cleaving" if the marriage was to be successful (see Mark 10:7, KJV). It was exactly the same for the disciples. If they were going to *cleave to* Jesus Christ, they would have to be willing to *leave for* Him. In their case, we are told they "left everything and followed Him" (Luke 5:11). The "everything" Luke mentions included, according to the other gospel writers, "their nets, the boat, their father, and the hired men."

Some of us may think it was no big deal for men like Peter, James, and John to leave their fathers. In fact, we might think it was about time they cut the apron strings. But this is to miss the point. These men knew that they were required by Moses to honor their father and mother, and in that society that meant, among other things, to look after them in their old age. Children were the only social security that first-century fathers possessed. For these men to leave their fathers and the business they had built together was a decision full of deep and lasting emotion. In fact, at a later date Peter grumbled, "We have left everything to follow You!" Jesus showed by His response that He knew what was on Peter's mind, stating specifically that those who had left "home or brothers or sisters or mother or father or children or fields" (Mark 10:28-29) would come out ahead in the long run.

Affections like a summer's garden can fill the life with joy and delight, but if left untended they can produce an ugly crop of weeds which choke the life and block the blessing. Some time ago a young woman came to me to talk about the fact that she seemed to have lost her joy in the Lord and to request prayer that it might be restored to her. When I endeavored to identify the cause of this sense of loss, she refused to get specific. Couldn't we just ask God to give her back her joy, she wondered? When I persisted, the woman tearfully admitted that she was living with her boyfriend and didn't want the church to know because she thought we might tell her it was wrong. We didn't need to tell her it was wrong. She knew that instinctively, but what she apparently did not know was that when one's affections are alienated away from the Master, one does not live in the conscious enjoyment of His presence. The decision to follow Christ presupposes the decision to forsake all that would alienate our affections from Him. The former is only operative when the latter is in effect.

The "everything" our Lord's disciples left behind causes concern for those who take the trouble to think about it. Does it mean that they literally deserted their families and took no further part in their care? This is highly unlikely because it would militate against all that Scripture teaches about responsibility for family. It is also helpful to note that the disciples did return for a time to their fishing, so the family business was apparently still intact. And we know that Peter certainly did not desert his wife because much later Paul commented on the fact that she was traveling with Peter in his itinerant ministry (see 1 Cor. 9:5).

What then does it mean that these disciples left everything, and what does it mean for modern disciples? As far as Jesus' original followers were concerned, their specific ministry necessitated that they be away from home for periods of time and that they could no longer make their living by fishing. For them, following Christ included a challenge to decide if what *He* wanted them to do rated ahead of what *they* wanted to do with their homes, families, and businesses. Or to put it another way: were they prepared to acknowledge His lordship of their lives in general with particular reference to these specific areas? The answer was yes, but it was not without a struggle—a continuing struggle.

The question for the modern disciple is, "How does this apply today?" The answer: "In much the same way!" For some people, the call of Christ requires a lifestyle where many of the comforts of home and the delights of family life are laid aside. Jill and I realized early in our marriage that Christ's call to us was that I should lay down a promising career in banking. Not that everybody with a promising career should do it, but for us it was necessary. Later we discovered that His call required me to be away on preaching missions for extended periods of time. Frequently I was asked by people who had invited me to minister in their country, "How can you justify being away from your family?"

"I can justify it because you apparently thought it was all right to ask me!" I replied.

"Yes, but how can you fulfill your biblical role of father and husband and be away from home so much?"

"I'll answer that if you can tell me how I can fulfill my calling as an international evangelist and stay at home!"

The point of tension between us was that these Christian brothers had their own ideas about home, family, and business, and they felt it necessary to impose their position on

me. To do this, however, was to overlook the fact that
Christ's call to discipleship means different things to different
people. But having said that, it must be understood that all
disciples are expected to place all their acquisitions at His
disposal in order that they might receive them back as stew-
ards of His resources.

When my wife graduated from college and started her
teaching career, she was thrilled to receive her first pay-
check. She took it to the bank and opened an account, but
was horrified to discover that there was no little box with her
name on it into which her money was placed until she went
to collect it. I explained to her that actually the bank didn't
even keep her money at the bank. "Then where is it?" she
asked.

"Well, it has been lent out to other people to pay for their
houses and cars."

"You mean they've let my money go and they don't know
where it is?"

"Well, yes and no. They don't know exactly where your
money is, but if you go in and ask for it they are required to
return it to you immediately. In the meantime they are putting
it to work."

As a banker I thought I understood banking until I tried to
explain it to my young wife, whose artistic and literary gifts
are outstanding but whose economic and accounting skills
are of a lesser caliber! But Jill did understand when I explained that stewardship works the same way. When we become Christ's disciples we leave everything, in the sense that
we gladly hand over all we have to Him. At that point He
returns those resources to us and we function as His stew-
ards. In practical terms this means that what we used to
regard as ours, we now reckon to be His. We put the resources to work in the interim until He calls upon us to
relinquish them for His purposes.

As we begin to grasp the implications of the call of Christ,
we can see how necessary it is that it comes to us gradually.
First we give Him our attention, then our affection, and then
our allegiance because we gladly recognize and appreciate
His attractiveness and authority.

Charlie Moore is a friend of mine who has ministered in Germany for many years. As a student in Florida, he decided that he would write out a detailed plan for his life, sign it, and then prayerfully ask the Lord to endorse it. But later he decided that was not the way God would work. So he got a blank sheet of paper, signed his name, and asked the Lord to fill in the details. If I know Charlie as I think I know him, that is exactly how he has lived his life for many years. He is a disciple of Jesus Christ skillfully disguised as a Lutheran pastor. ♦

Jesus Came Calling

WHEN THE TIME CAME for Jesus to embark on His public ministry, having completed thirty years of preparation, He wasted no time putting His team of disciples together. There is no way that the Twelve could have had any idea of the far-reaching implications of their response to His call. Never in a thousand years would they have believed that their names would become internationally recognizable centuries after their decease, oceans away from the only world they knew. They would have laughed incredulously if they had been told that God would commit to them the task of discipling the nations. But that was what Jesus had in mind when He went calling.

The call of Christ to His disciples always includes two ingredients—namely, invitation and challenge. "Come to Me, all who are weary and heavy-laden" (Matt. 11:28, NASB) indicates the scope of the invitation. "All" weary and overburdened people are welcome to find rest through a relationship with Him. "If any man is thirsty, let him come to Me and drink" (John 7:37, NASB) echoes a similar all-embracing offer, promising refreshment to the parched soul. "Come, follow Me, and I will make you fishers of men" (Matt. 4:19) reiterates the invitation, this time with the promise that followers will be recycled into an entirely different lifestyle and purpose. Rest, refreshment, and recycling are perennially attractive themes to the tired, the empty, and the frustrated people whose lives have littered the landscapes of the first century and of succeeding generations.

We should not overlook the rather obvious fact that each invitation is to *a relationship with* Jesus Christ. "Come to Me," He calls repeatedly. The original disciples were not attracted to a burgeoning movement, for there was none. As time went on, some of them got the idea that perhaps the Master would become successful in a bid for political power, and two of them—James and John—apparently began to think about the upholstery they would choose for their respective thrones. But they were quickly informed that there would be no such throne for the Master and most definitely no thrones for them.

History holds many examples of the process that starts with a man, becomes a movement, and ends a monument. While many empty cathedrals, dusty tombstones, and failed ministries might suggest, to those who wish to believe it, that Christ has become just another outmoded and irrelevant relic, the fact remains that never have there been so many disciples of Christ than as there are now. Jesus' invitation has been accepted by more people in the present generation than in any previous generation and the reason is not hard to find: He has always delivered exactly what He promised. That's why His attraction is as powerful today as ever, His impact as great now as in days long gone by.

Modern-day disciples on factory floors and in surgical suites are not part of a moribund movement struggling for survival. They are intimately related to the Christ who invites them now to share His risen life through His Spirit, in much the same way that He invited the Twelve to share His earthly life on the dusty roads of the Middle East. The invitation today is essentially the same: "Come to Me."

But the call of Jesus Christ also includes an element of challenge. "Come to Me" is linked immediately with the phrase, "Follow Me." As we saw in chapter 3, Greek disciples followed their teacher as he practiced what we now call peripatetic teaching (that means he walked around while he was doing it!). Likewise, the disciples of Jesus literally walked after Him as they journeyed, and we know that He taught them as He walked and they followed. But there can be little doubt that "following" meant more than just physically moving along a pace or two behind the Lord wherever He went. It meant and still means the willingness to accept His leadership and obey His instructions. This truth comes through clearly in Christ's final instructions to His disciples, when He commissioned them to "make disciples of all nations ... *teaching them to obey everything I have commanded you*" (Matt. 28:19-20, italics added).

Original disciples found something so irresistibly winsome about Jesus that when the invitation came, they responded joyfully. But they saw something so powerfully commanding about Him that when the challenge to follow was issued, they promptly obeyed. Disciples need to know the Master well enough to be able to recognize His beauty *and* His authority, for this knowledge alone leads to an adequate response to the call to discipleship.

Jon McGlocklin, who played for the Milwaukee Bucks from 1965 to 1976, was known as one of the "purest shooters" in the National Basketball Association. With his clean-cut good looks and friendly demeanor he was immensely popular around the league and the city he had made his home. Having enjoyed watching him play on many occasions, I was delighted to meet him personally one day at Chicago's O'Hare Airport. The mutual friend who introduced us, Eddie Doucette, was himself a new believer, and showed his babe-in-Christ eagerness by saying to me in Jon's presence, "You should tell him what you've been telling me. He sure needs it." Jon stiffened visibly, so I tried to recover some lost ground by quipping, "I never met anyone who didn't need help."

Turning on his heel, Jon retorted as he walked hurriedly away, "Well, you just met your first one, Reverend."

Months later I met Jon again. This time he rather shyly said to me, "I've made some changes since we talked the last time."

"Tell me about it," I replied.

He recounted how for many weeks he had been confronted with the reality of Christ's life in some of his friends, including Eddie. And on his own, Jon had started reading a Bible and thinking through what he was learning about the Lord. One night he checked into a hotel and, while he waited for his bags to be brought to the room, switched on the television. He wasn't watching with any great attention when the young baggage porter arrived and, noting it was a religious program, said, "Oh, are you a Christian?"

Jon, not at all eager to get into a religious discussion with a stranger at that late hour, muttered something noncommittal; but the young man persisted. He told Jon how he had become a disciple of Jesus Christ two years earlier, then asked, "Would you like me to pray for you?"

"No thanks, that's not necessary," Jon replied, but then quickly added, "OK. If you want to."

When the porter left the room a minute or two later, Jon fell to his knees and cried out to God his desire to become Christ's disciple.

Over the years, Jon McGlocklin and I have become close friends, and I thoroughly enjoy seeing him grow in the Lord. But one thing sticks out in my mind concerning the way he became a disciple. As he puts it, "I hear all these stories about people's lives falling apart after they've tried everything, and then as a last resort they turn to the Lord. But my life wasn't falling apart. My wife, Pam, and I have a super relationship; the kids are doing well. My playing career is over, but I have good opportunities in sports broadcasting and other business ventures. In fact, everything is coming up roses. I didn't commit my life to Christ as a last resort. I committed myself to Him because it was the right thing to do." In other words, Jon took his time considering the person of Christ presented in the pages of Scripture and in the lives of other disciples, then decided that he too would become a follower.

Without in any way wishing to detract from the precious experiences of those who come to Christ out of desperation, we do need to emphasize that sooner or later everyone has to decide whether or not to follow Jesus on the basis of who He is as well as on the basis of what He offers. If this does not happen, the possibility always exists that once Christ has met the need which He was asked to address, He might slide into relative obscurity. But for the person who is attracted to Him and renders deep allegiance to Him, this is not a danger. While they might not share the athletic talents of Jon McGlocklin, a disciple of Jesus Christ skillfully disguised as a former NBA all-star, they very definitely share the same delight in who Jesus is and who they are in Him—namely, disciples.   ◆

You Can't Move Without Changing

I'VE OFTEN WONDERED how much Simon understood about what he was getting into when he first met the Lord. It could have been quite unnerving to be told, "You are Simon son of John. You will be called Cephas (which, when translated, is Peter)" (John 1:42).

Granted, some people hate their names and would gladly have them changed. But other people like their names very much and aren't about to surrender them. Indeed, not a few modern young women insist not only on retaining their maiden names when they get married but ask their husbands to assume both surnames. So, for example, when John Smith marries Jane Black, the result is John and Jane Black-Smith!

Yes, there's pride in a name, but there's also meaning in a name. Simon is a derivation of the Hebrew name Simeon. Presumably Simon's parents thought they would like their newborn boy to bear the name of one of the twelve tribes of Israel. But their choice is open to question because Simeon was not the greatest role model for a young man. Take it from his father Jacob, who summed up Simeon and his brother Levi as follows:

> Their swords are weapons of violence.
>   Let me not enter their council,
>   let me not join their assembly,

for they have killed men in their anger
and hamstrung oxen as they pleased.
Cursed be their anger, so fierce,
and their fury, so cruel!
(Gen. 49:5-7)

Without wanting to load a lot of ancestral baggage on Simon, I think it is not inappropriate to recognize that in renaming him Jesus was saying something about the changes that would be necessary in the life of His disciple.

A striking similarity existed in the temperaments of these two Simons. Both demonstrated a tendency to unstable recklessness that could give way to violence under the right conditions. If Jacob was wary of entering into his son's council, the same could certainly be said for Jesus' reluctance to follow His erratic disciple Simon's advice. And while the New Testament Simon didn't commit anything close to the treacherous and bloody massacre of the Shechemites, of which his ancestral namesake was guilty (see Gen. 34), he did show that he was not averse to using a sword with some degree of enthusiasm, if not expertise, in the Garden of Gethsemane. Clearly, some changes were necessary.

Change *from* is one thing. Change *to* is another thing entirely. Simon's new name in Aramaic was to be Cephas; the Greek equivalent is Petros, from which we get Peter. Both the Aramaic and Greek names mean "rock"—indicating not only the direction but also the extent of the change that discipleship would mean to Peter. From Simon to Rocky was a transformation of major proportions.

That there was little evidence of this change during the three years of Christ's earthly ministry speaks of two things: first, the immense patience of the great Disciplemaker, the Lord Jesus, and second, the slowness with which major change in human character is accomplished. But even a cursory reading of Peter's epistles shows how this erstwhile unstable man later did indeed become a rock to the believers who had been scattered throughout the Roman provinces, and for whom life had become difficult and would probably get much worse. To them he wrote, "And the God of all grace,

who called you to His eternal glory in Christ, after you have
suffered a little while, will Himself restore you and make you
strong, firm, and steadfast" (1 Peter 5:10). "Strong, firm, and
steadfast" was not the stuff of which the two Simons were
made, but they were the qualities of the Peter whom the
Great Discipler had fashioned from such unpromising
material.

I once had dinner with a world famous golf course architect, and I was particularly intrigued to find out how she went
about her work. We had looked at pictures of the land from
which some of the great courses have been fashioned. In
their primitive state these tracts seemed most unpromising.
But the skilled architect had done her homework. She had
checked not only the topography, but the soil, the water supply, the drainage, and the climate. Detailed measurements,
innumerable plans, and various scenarios had been presented
and modified before the earth movers arrived on the scene.
Once they did, the result looked like World War III. But as the
pictorial records showed, little by little the scene changed as
the work progressed, and eventually a beautiful golf course
emerged. Yet, she added, the work was never really finished—because if constant care were not lavished upon it,
the weeds and the vines would take over, and the course
would all but disappear.

As we have already noted, when Peter was confronted on
an intimate level with the majestic power of the Lord Jesus,
his instinctive response was to ask Him to leave. This was a
clear admission of sensitivity to his own unsatisfactory (i.e.,
sinful) condition and the perfection of the Master. There was
no way in his own thinking at that moment that the two could
ever coexist. So the only solution was that the Lord should
leave him alone, to live the rest of his days in confused and
dissatisfied failure.

But there was another solution of which he was not aware
at that time. Instead of Jesus leaving and Simon staying as he
was, Jesus would stay and change Simon into Peter. It is at
this point—recognition of the need for and the desirability of
change—that true discipleship gets under way. But even
where there is a recognition of need and an admission of

desirability, there is still the need for a willingness to be changed.

When Ronald Reagan was campaigning for President in 1980, he promised to get big government off our backs, to trim the "fat" from the federal budget, and many other exciting things. On the strength of these and similar promises, he was elected with great enthusiasm by the majority of the voters of the United States. Some realized that the proposed changes would not be without cost and might never happen; idealists, however, saw only the goal and not the process. Most of the people I talked to wanted change, but they didn't want anything to affect them adversely. This attitude was cleverly portrayed in a cartoon which pictured the President, dressed as a surgeon, standing over John Doe lying on an operating table. As the surgeon-President approached him, scalpel in hand, the hapless John Doe was saying, "Cut and slash, Doctor, but don't make me bleed."

When I joined Britain's Royal Marines as an idealistic, adventuresome eighteen-year-old, I was aware that they would make some changes in me. But I had no idea the extent of those changes. I've often wondered if I would have volunteered had I known in advance about the gruesome details which go into making a banker into a Marine. The answer is probably no—except when I'm with other ex-Marines, of course—but it's a purely hypothetical question, because one never knows in advance what he is going to go through even though he may have a general idea. Similarly, I am convinced that disciples of Jesus Christ need to be aware that change is necessary, painful, and inevitable, but there is no way they can or should know what they will be called to go through. Just as long as they are willing to take it a step at a time, they will not come to much harm.

Perhaps the inevitability of change may have escaped some of us. By definition, disciples "follow." That means they go where they have never been or at least where they aren't at that particular moment! To put it another way, they progress.

One day a man spent the afternoon pouring a concrete driveway. After finishing the job and taking a warm shower he settled down to read the paper only to see a small boy carefully walking up the wet cement. Jumping up from his seat, he rushed to the door and told the youngster exactly what he thought of him. At that critical moment the vicar walked by, heard the commotion, and commented to the irate man, "I thought you loved small boys." To which the man replied, "I do in the abstract, but not in the concrete."

Unfortunately, we all love things more in the abstract than the concrete. Change, for example. Jesus told Simon Peter and his brother, "I will make you fishers of men" (Mark 1:17). Note the emphasis: *I* will make *you*. Now my reading of Simon Peter is that he was a self-made man who, like most self-made men, was rather proud of his creation. He certainly gave plenty of indication during his three-year stint with the Lord that he was opinionated, strong-willed, and determined. Therefore, the thought of someone other than himself making something out of him necessitated a marked change in attitude. On numerous occasions I have talked to men, particularly, who have resisted the idea that they should allow anyone to take over their lives and effect changes therein. Not even the Lord! I suspect the reason is that we have swallowed the myth of our own independence and resist anything that might suggest we are in any way dependent—even though all the evidence points unequivocally in that direction. Disciples need to be willing to have their attitudes changed at this point.

Jesus also indicated to His first followers that there would be a marked change in the direction of their lives if they got into a disciple-teacher relationship with Him. He would make them "fishers of men." They knew how to be fishers of fish even though they didn't always do very well at it. But then all fishermen have their days when the fish don't cooperate in committing suicide. To move from fishing for fish to fishing for men may have sounded exciting, but in all probability it sounded somewhat unnerving too. They had never done it before! What if they were no good at it? Fish didn't answer back when you tried to catch them, but if the Galileans they knew were anything to go by, they would not only argue but punch you out if they didn't appreciate what you were saying! And what about the hours and the travel? Would it necessitate them spending a lot of time away from home?

If these questions seem fanciful, I admit that they are, as related to Simon and Andrew. But they are not at all fanciful when related to the people I have talked to about being disciples. In fact, these are the exact reactions I have heard repeatedly when I mention the changes in plans that the Lord may wish to introduce into Christians' lives.

But let's face it. If we're going to change, we have to be willing to move into new and therefore challenging areas. This challenge produces apprehension because we don't know what we're getting into. And the natural response to apprehension is to shy away from whatever is causing the apprehension—unless of course, we remember that the change is to be introduced and effected by the Lord Himself. We are in His hands, under His care, slotted into His program, covered and secured by His grace.

After living in the United States for a few years, I returned to London, to participate in meetings with the Billy Graham Evangelistic Team. As I was walking from the meeting place back to my hotel, I bumped into a young man named Rob Whittaker. We had not seen each other for three or four years.

"What on earth are you doing here?" I asked.

"Funny you should say that," he replied. "I was just going to ask you the same thing."

We exchanged news of each other's activities and Rob told me that, having completed his degree at the London Bible College, he had tried unsuccessfully to find a place of ministry. So he had returned to his hometown and was working for the Parks and Gardens Department.

"I can't believe you're doing that," I said.

"What else can I do if nobody wants me in their church?"

"You could always start one of your own," I suggested without any great degree of conviction.

"What do you mean?" he answered with immediate surprise and interest. "How do you start a church?"

"Well, you just go out there and beat the bushes and find people who need the Lord, lead them on in the knowledge of Him, and form them into a church." I must admit I had not expected his response, so my answer was not at all prepared. No matter. The Spirit was working.

"Why didn't I think of that? That's a great idea," Rob exclaimed.

We talked for some time about what might be involved in planting a church; then he went his way and I went mine. Not many months later Rob wrote me one of the most exciting letters I have ever received. He told countless moving and often hilarious stories about the people he had been meeting. He talked about their reactions and responses and about the little church that had been formed. Years later the church is no longer little and Rob's ministry has been acknowledged in many parts of the British Isles and on the continent of Europe. The key factor, however, was that at one point of his life, standing on a sidewalk in the middle of London, Rob confronted the possibility that the Lord wanted to move him from what he was doing, lead him into unknown territory, and make him into something he had never dreamed he could be. Rob Whittaker was a disciple of Jesus Christ skillfully disguised as a grass cutter and plant planter until he changed garb and became a disciple who is now an expert fisher of men. ◆

But What About You?

JESUS WAS CAUSING quite a sensation. Wherever He went, the people were discussing Him. The disciples, no doubt, enjoyed being in the middle of the action. They talked to the people who were so anxious to learn all they could about this mysterious, wonderful Person who had walked unbidden into their lives. As the Twelve answered the crowd's questions, they themselves became minor celebrities—even if the glory was reflected glory.

One of the most fascinating subjects for discussion and conjecture was the identity of this carpenter from Nazareth. It was clear to everybody that He was no ordinary man. Some thought He was John the Baptist returned to life. No doubt this was a most appealing thought to the crowds, if not to Herod. Others who had a keener sense of history and prophecy thought perhaps He was the great Prophet Elijah resurrected from the dead. Some, equally convinced that He was a prophet, were satisfied to think that He might be a more contemporary representative of that intrepid band of men who had periodically marched with dramatic effect across the stage of Israel's history. A common theme ran through all their speculations. He was unusual; He was dramatically calling the people's attention to God; and He had a message which He backed up with breathtaking evidences of supernatural power.

As the disciples trudged along the road en route to Caesarea Philippi one day, the Master asked them, "Who do people say I am?" (Mark 8:27) They quickly gave Him the information they had gleaned from their discussions with the people and no doubt felt very pleased with themselves that they were sufficiently in touch with the situation. Jesus previously had let them know that He was unhappy with their lack of spiritual understanding, so this would be a boost to their flagging confidence. At least they knew something!

If the Twelve felt good about their responses, they were not given much time to enjoy their success. Jesus immediately challenged them to answer the question, "But what about you? Who do you say I am?" (v. 29)

This is one of the most important questions any person can be called upon to answer. And strangely, it is one of those questions which even religious people often seem reluctant to field. The reluctance may be caused by a fear of being challenged to some kind of theological debate or a feeling of inability to articulate properly. Both of these concerns can be readily overcome. But there is a more serious aspect to this reluctance, and that is the possibility that those who claim a religious experience may in reality have little or no relationship to Christ.

Many years ago I was invited to preach in a small church in northern England, and because I was unsure of its location, I arrived about half an hour earlier than necessary. Fortunately, the church janitor was there. He took me to a small vestry sparsely furnished with a table and two hard chairs. We sat down together and he began to tell me all about the church. He had obviously spent a major part of his life serving this parish and was thoroughly acquainted with the minute details of the building's architecture: its deficiencies, decay, and repairs. Having filled me in on those details, he turned his attention to the people. He seemed to know everything worth knowing about all of them and some things not worth knowing. Next, he gave me the life stories of the ministers who had pastored the church over the previous fifty years. I listened as attentively as I could to his enthusiastic recital of the life and times of his church and, at last, as I had not said a word the entire time, I thought I should make some response to him. So I said, "Tell me about the Lord Jesus." If I had suddenly kicked him on the ankle under the table he could not have looked more startled. Jumping up from the chair, he said, "Come on, it's time we were getting into the service," and without so much as a glance in my direction, he rushed out of the room. Without in any way presuming to suggest I know the spiritual condition of this gentleman who was deeply devoted to his church, it goes without saying that Jesus *does* ask His followers to answer the question, "But what about *you?* Who do *you* say I am?"

In our church we hold a class for people who wish to join our congregation. We spend time teaching the basics of the faith, elaborating on the specifics of our church's identity, history, and objectives. We also ask each potential member to explain his or her experience of Christ. To many, this has proved a great challenge, and some have declined to respond. When this happens, we talk with the individuals concerned, seeking to identify the causes of their reluctance. In some instances, it has been nothing but shyness, but in others we have discovered a commitment that is shallow at best and possibly nonexistent at worst. In the latter case, the reason that these men and women have nothing to say is simply because nothing is there to articulate. But as we take seriously the call to articulate our personal convictions concerning the Master, however falteringly, our hearts are stretched and our faith is encouraged. The importance of this truth can be seen when we return to the conversation between the Master and His disciples.

Peter, ever ready to express an opinion, quickly responded to the Master's question, saying, "You are the Christ" (Mark 8:29). By this he meant that he recognized that Jesus was specially anointed by God to fulfill a unique mission. The prophets had promised for centuries that Jehovah would send His special envoy to restore the fortunes of Israel and bring blessing to the Gentiles as well. As a well-versed Jew, Peter was keenly aware of this promise and had no doubts that he was walking the dusty roads of Israel as a personally called disciple of this special envoy. He was convinced and not the least bit reluctant to voice his conviction. Flushed with the added triumph of being able to answer a deeply significant question correctly, after giving the Master the information for which He had asked, Peter must have been devastated when Jesus then instructed the disciples not to tell anyone! (v. 30) Why would this be so? Isn't it inconsistent if the Master asks His disciples to say who they think He is and when they do, He tells them to keep quiet about it?

The answer to this seeming inconsistency is not hard to find. Jesus immediately thereafter began to teach the disciples that He would "suffer many things and be rejected by the elders, chief priests, and teachers of the Law, and that He must be killed and after three days rise again" (v. 31). Peter was absolutely right about Jesus being the Christ, but he was absolutely wrong about the kind of Christ Jesus was. If Peter had been allowed to propagate his understanding of who Jesus was, the damage would have been considerable. Indeed, Peter reacted so violently to Jesus' statement about His coming death that he actually took the Master "aside and began to rebuke Him" (v. 32). This in itself shows how much this "infant" disciple had yet to learn!

When I was born in 1930, my mother had a long, difficult delivery through which she suffered considerably. As a result, I appeared on the scene looking much the worse for wear. She told me rather shyly one day that when they placed me in her arms, she looked at the misshapen head and blotched face of her long-awaited firstborn and cried, "Oh, I didn't want a baby like that!" Fortunately, I didn't quite catch what she said at the time, so I suffered no lasting psychological damage—even though some of my friends say that when they look at me today they understand exactly what she meant!

I think Peter must have thought something similar when he looked at the self-portrait the Master was painting, and perhaps in his heart he was saying, "Oh, I didn't want a Christ like that!" Sensing that the Master may have misunderstood His mission, Peter hastened to eradicate from His mind the depressed and negative thoughts about rejection and death. In Peter's scenario, the Christ would be a charismatic, vivacious leader who would win the hearts of the people, rid

Israel of the hated Roman yoke, and restore the land to the splendor it enjoyed when David and Solomon ruled and reigned. And therein lay Peter's problem. He had manufactured his own Christ.

This is a problem of great magnitude even today. There is no shortage of "disciples" of "Christ" but when the "Christ" of these "disciples" is evaluated, he bears little resemblance to the Christ of Scripture. For example, I counsel with people who tell me what they are planning to do in certain areas of their lives. If I find it necessary to point out to them that the Lord has expressly forbidden the kind of behavior they are proposing, the response has been, "Well, I know that, but He wants me to be happy. And as this would make me happy, I don't think He will mind!" Variations on this theme are becoming increasingly prevalent, mainly because our contemporary society had bought into an approach to life where rightness and wrongness are determined by subjective criteria, not objective truth. Feeling good and looking good have superseded being good and doing good. The danger of this approach is clear. To follow a "Christ" of the imagination is to commit one's life to a phantom.

Suppose Peter had been right. His "Christ" would have been a widely accepted leader who most certainly would not be crucified and therefore would find it neither necessary nor possible to rise again from the dead. The result would have been a much more amicable experience for all concerned, with the unfortunate result that there would have been no redemption through His shed blood, no triumph over sin and death and hell, and no answer to the deepest need of the human race—the forgiveness of sin and reconciliation with the Father. Fortunately, Peter was wrong, and so are all those who depart from the Christ of revelation to a Christ of imagination!

Disciples of Christ need to remember that He was rejected in His day by three categories of people who represented the major decision-making segments of society. Times have not changed. The elders were the political leaders, the chief priests the religious leaders, and the teachers the moral leaders. It was unthinkable to Peter that Jesus could succeed as

Christ without being accepted and embraced by the formidable forces of contemporary politics, religion, and morality. But that was exactly how it was going to be! The same is true today. Whenever attempts are made to enroll Jesus as a card-carrying member of a political party, or to baptize Him as a member of an exclusive religious system, or to seek His endorsement for any man-made moral philosophy, those well-meaning people fail to remember that ultimately He stands outside these structures and in judgment upon them because of their flawed humanness.

In the same way, any attempt to diminish the significance of Jesus' death serves only to rob humanity of its only hope. Many advocates of Christ see His teachings and example, quite rightly, as the truth which they should seek to emulate. But they refuse to accept the fact that by teaching and example, He showed our sinfulness in even starker terms and highlighted the absolute necessity of His atoning death. For them to refuse a rejected and redemptive Christ might produce a more acceptable Christ. But it also would serve only to produce an impotent deliverer full of truth and good intentions, but devoid of power to change the hearts of men and bring them back to God.

It is obvious that if Peter was having problems with the idea of the Christ being crucified (and we would probably have reacted in an identical fashion!), there was no way he could begin to grasp the idea of Him rising again from the dead. Given what he knew at that time, it is not difficult to see that the concept was utterly incomprehensible to him and therefore to be rejected!

Which of us has not found ourselves in the same position of consciously or unconsciously rejecting that which we have found incomprehensible about Christ? But to do so is to limit Him to the confines of our intellectual grasp. And the result, of course, is a pygmy Christ (with all due respect to our considerable intellects!).

If Peter had problems with the rejected, redemptive, risen Lord with whom he was being confronted, try to imagine how he reacted when he learned that this same Jesus would come "in His Father's glory with the holy angels" (Mark 8:38).

There was such vastness to the Christ standing before him that he could not even begin to think of Him reigning on such a scale.

Peter knew what he knew, but he didn't know how much he didn't know. And some things he "knew" were not right at all. But give him credit—he was open; he was learning; he was responding as best he knew how; he was making progress. And he loved the Lord he didn't necessarily understand. In short, he was a disciple.

C.S. Lewis, the distinguished scholar who taught at both Oxford and Cambridge, had a long spiritual journey which took him from atheism to commitment to Christ. At different stages of the journey, he passed through romanticism, idealism, and theism, before eventually arriving at a place where he could confidently identify with the Christ of Scripture. And in identifying, he began to articulate brilliantly what he had discovered. He was a disciple of Jesus Christ skillfully disguised as a medieval scholar, so it is not surprising that he was brilliant and elegant in his defense of the faith. Fortunately, that kind of literary ability is not necessary, but that kind of commitment and statement is. Today the question still stands, "But what about *you?* Who do *you* say Jesus is?" ◆

Boy, Am I Confused!

I HEARD ABOUT A MAN who wore a button on his lapel with the letters B.A.I.K.

Someone asked him, "What does B.A.I.K. mean?"

"It means, 'Boy am I confused!'"

"But you don't spell *confused* with a K."

"You don't?" the man responded. "Boy, I'm more confused than I thought!"

It's one thing to be confused. It's another thing to be confused and not know it. But what about the poor people who are confused, and know they're confused, but have no idea of how confused they are? (Did I confuse you?)

Certainly the disciples of Jesus had gotten a lot of things right about Him and had acted courageously on their convictions. They had determined that He was the "Lamb of God" who had come to take away the sin of the world. As they had watched Christ in action around the shores of the lake that they called home, they had decided He was worthy of their allegiance. When He had come to them specifically and challenged them to "follow Him" and be made into "fishers of men," they had responded with rare enthusiasm and bravery.

But they soon found out that they were expected to be more than His entourage, meekly following Him wherever He went, passively listening to His sermons and observing His miracles. Jesus had every intention of putting them to work.

He paired them off, gave them "authority over evil spirits" (Mark 6:7), and sent them out to teach. No doubt the disciples had seen how the Lord had addressed the crushing physical, emotional, and spiritual needs of the people with a ministry of healing, exorcism, and teaching; so they carefully followed His example. The results were exciting and startling. People were healed, delivered from demonic oppression, and effectively confronted with the necessity for repentance.

There is no enthusiasm like that of the new believer whose faith is so fresh. New horizons have been unveiled; a sense of previously unknown peace prevails; a burden has been lifted; and it is the most natural thing in the world to tell everyone about it. Of course, there is danger in new enthusiasm for it often invites reaction by virtue of its overt and often extreme exuberance. Imagine a new convert, full of enthusiasm, thrust into a ministry where he actually exorcises demons, heals sick people, and sees people coming to repentance! It is not difficult to understand the state of euphoria in which he lives and the excitement that pervades his new walk!

The disciples returned to the Master and gave Him a breathless report of all that they had done, said, and observed. He wisely said to them, "Come with Me by yourselves to a quiet place and get some rest" (Mark 6:31). With the adrenalin flowing, who needs a rest? With a world full of needy people, who needs to get alone for quiet? With momentum on your side, who wants to take a break? But of course these men were disciples and disciples have to learn!

No doubt you have watched distance races where a couple of runners immediately go to the front of the pack and set a fast pace. These front runners are called "rabbits." That is, they are in the race to set a quick pace for the benefit of the other runners, but they themselves have no intention of finishing. They go off in a blaze of glory and fizzle like fireworks on the Fourth of July.

This is exactly what can, and sometimes does happen to disciples who start at a terrific pace, quickly run out of spiritual gas, and finally drop out of the race. But it doesn't have to happen. Disciples need to take a break to take in, if they are to learn how to give out.

So off the Twelve went with the Master to take their well-deserved break! Unfortunately, the crowds didn't get the message, so they crashed the party. Five thousand men and their families!

There was something pathetic about the crowds that deeply touched the Lord. They were rushing around like shepherdless sheep, trying to find satisfaction without knowing where to look, searching for answers without being sure of the questions, and, like sheep, putting themselves at risk through their wanderings. (What an apt description of contemporary society too!) So the Lord forgot about the quiet day off and taught the people right through until evening. Everybody forgot about food except the disciples, who were beginning to get a little nervous about managing the crowds. They made a very practical suggestion, "Send the people away so they can go to the surrounding countryside and villages and buy themselves something to eat" (Mark 6:36).

"You give them something to eat," was the totally inexplicable retort from the Master! (v. 37)

Philip, a practical quick-thinker, calculated that it would take at least "eight months of a man's wages" to feed a crowd that size and he and the others didn't seem too enthusiastic about pooling their resources to feed a crowd they didn't invite in the first place. Yet the Lord told them to check for food anyway. Andrew apparently was the only one who came up with anything at all, and the best he could do was to find a little boy clutching his lunch of five small loaves and two fish. When Andrew appeared with the boy and his lunch, he was obviously embarrassed with the results of his search, exclaiming, "How far will they go among so many?" (John 6:9) Well might he ask, and we would have asked the same thing, assuming we had done as well. The answer was not long in arriving, for in the Master's hands these apparently inadequate supplies proved to be more than enough.

To the utter astonishment of the disciples, who had recently experienced their own brand of miracles, Jesus fed the multitude and the ground was littered with leftovers. Presumably endorsing a "Keep Galilee Tidy" campaign, they picked up the fragments and not incidentally filled twelve baskets.

One for each bemused disciple!

If the disciples wanted an explanation of these remarkable events, they were disappointed because as soon as the crowds dispersed they were ushered into a boat and told to go home while the Lord spent some much needed time in prayer. But the fishermen soon encountered a Galilean storm. They knew they were in for a long night if not a watery grave (or both), but they had no idea of what was really about to happen. About three o'clock in the morning they saw what they thought was a ghost floating over the angry surface of the waves. This served only to add terror to exhaustion. The "Ghost," however, spoke to them and said, "Take courage! It is I. Don't be afraid" (Mark 6:50), then climbed into the boat and revealed Himself to them. Mark, in his gospel, adds not surprisingly, "They were completely amazed," but then most surprisingly continues, "for they had not understood about the loaves; their hearts were hardened" (vv. 51-52). So in addition to being terrorstruck and exhausted, these unfortunate men were still confused.

Mark's point appears to be that if the disciples had grasped the significance of the loaves, they would not have been surprised about Christ walking on water. But notice that he attributes their confusion to the fact that "their hearts were hardened." To what were their hearts hardened? When the Lord identified Himself to them on the waves, He said literally, "I am." This could mean simply "It's Me," or it could be a title designed to trigger the disciples' memories to the great statements of Jehovah's self-revelation to Moses. There He said, "I am who I am. . . . Say to the Israelites: 'I AM has sent me to you'" (Ex. 3:14).

Given the circumstances in which the Lord made the statement and given Mark's comment about the disciples' confusion and hardness of heart, it would seem that the disciples had decided that they would believe some things about Jesus, but would draw the line at believing that He was a manifestation of Jehovah the great I AM.

Now, of course, it is so easy to fault these men with the benefit of 20/20 hindsight and the marked advantage of sitting in a warm room in a comfortable chair rather than in a rocking boat on a vicious sea. Nevertheless, the lesson for us appears to be that even disciples can decide what they are and are not going to believe. But if they do this, the result will be confusion in their walk of discipleship.

That this was the case becomes evident when we note that in the next chapter Mark records the Lord's question to them, "Are you so dull?" (7:18), and then in the following chapter, "Do you still not see or understand? Are your hearts hardened? Do you have eyes but fail to see, and ears but fail to hear?" (8:17-18) Remember that in addition to the disciples' witnessing the feeding of the 5,000 with five loaves and two fish, they had also seen the Lord feed about 4,000 men with seven loaves and a few fish. No wonder it was so disconcerting to Him that they were still confused.

But what exactly was the nature of their confusion? Put in simple terms, it seemed to be that they often operated on an entirely different wavelength from the Lord. For instance, after the feeding miracles, they were on a journey and someone realized that they had brought only one loaf of bread. So what's new? Given their intense interest in eating, the Lord took this opportunity to warn them about the "yeast of the Pharisees and that of Herod" (Mark 8:15). Jesus apparently thought that it was reasonable to assume that the disciples would be in touch with His thinking and respond accordingly, what with John the Baptist having been recently killed by Herod and the Pharisees having recently stepped up their campaign against Him. Instead, they thought He was upset that somebody had blown it by forgetting the bread!

We may find this whole episode amusing or incredible, but a moment's thought will suffice to show that missing the point is a common problem for disciples then and now. The really disappointing thing both for the Lord and would-be disciples is that this kind of confusion is all too close to the confusion experienced by nondisciples. Remember when the Lord talked to the Samaritan woman at Sychar? He explained to her about living water and all she could think about was how He would get it out of the well without a bucket! (see John 4:11) To her, He talked about living water and she was worried about buckets; to the disciples, He talked about spiritual danger and they talked about forgetting lunch. But the underlying problem was that neither were on the right wavelength because they had hardened their hearts somewhere along the line. Progress had come to a screeching halt, and they may not even have realized that it had happened.

We started this chapter relating the disciples' exciting experiences as they went out in pairs and saw God use them to bless others. It is ironic that such euphoria gave way to confusion. And it must have been hard for the disciples to realize that the Lord's approval of their ministry efforts was tempered by a marked degree of dissatisfaction concerning their lack of inner progress.

There has to be a lesson here for modern-day disciples. I suspect that the Twelve had learned enough about the Lord to become equipped to do the kind of things they liked doing. Exorcising and preaching and healing were exciting and rewarding and fun! They had garnered a degree of fame and recognition. No doubt they were in great demand, so what else did they need? They had enough to do well enough; they knew enough to rate highly enough. So why bother thinking and learning and wrestling with the hard things? They were doing great, right? What they didn't know was that they weren't doing as well as they fondly imagined; and if they didn't get things straight about the Lord, they would end up flat on their evangelical noses, where many a modern-day disciple has landed in a cloud of dust.

I am reminded of the kid who got a new bike and quickly learned to ride. He disappeared around the block and returned at great speed shouting, "Look, Mom, no hands!"

The next time around: "Look, Mom, no feet!"

The third time around: "Look, Mom, no teeth!"

Those disciples who think they know it all, or think they know enough, are the ones who end up confused because they have failed to deepen in their knowledge of Christ. If, in addition, they have gained positions of acceptance and prominence beyond their ability to handle, they are in danger of losing their spiritual teeth. They, of all people, need to remember that *disciple* means "learner," however one is disguised. ◆

Facing the Issues

OSTRICHES ARE SAID TO bury their heads in the sand when they see something they don't like. When I visited an ostrich farm in South Africa, I asked one of the farmers if this were true. Without answering, he took the long neck of the bird he was riding (yes, he was riding it!) and began to twist it around so that it looked like a tangled length of hose. Releasing the unfortunate bird's neck, which promptly unraveled and returned to its former state, he said, "There's no way an ostrich can bury its head in the sand because it has no bones in its neck!" I was distressed that I had been using an incorrect analogy for years and even more distressed about the treatment of the bird! Nevertheless, I still think it is appropriate to talk about people burying their heads in the sand when they refuse to confront issues.

Whatever else might be said about the disciples of Jesus, they were not "ostriches." It is true that they were learning slowly, but such was their relationship with the Master that they could hardly avoid the issues He habitually raised. One of the most frightening issues was highlighted in the awesome confrontation between Jesus and Peter, recorded in Mark 8:31-38. The Master no doubt recognized that Peter meant well when he tried to dissuade Him from speaking about His forthcoming rejection and death. True, Peter had "rebuked" the Lord (the word is the same one used to describe the Lord's rebuke of the demons), an action that was as inappropriate as it was typical. But the Master's response was brutally to the point: "Out of My sight, Satan!" (Mark 8:33) How Peter survived that blast, I cannot imagine.

Peter had unwittingly raised an issue that most people would rather bypass. The issue? That men and women can do the devil's work for him. For Peter to suggest that the Master should not die was to suggest that He deviate from the path of obedience, which is exactly what the devil wants people to do all the time. We know that Jesus was "tempted in every way, just as we are" (Heb. 4:15), so it is not unreasonable to assume that Jesus saw Peter's well-meaning-but-totally-unacceptable proposition as the devil's handiwork. If that is the case, then there is an issue here that must not be ignored. It doesn't take a lot of maturity to know that anyone who puts a drink in front of a recovering alcoholic is putting temptation in his way. Some people at the annual office party might think it is fun, but if exposing people to temptation is the devil's work, there is nothing funny about it. Many a young man has encouraged a young woman to overcome her moral convictions concerning sexual behavior by telling her that if she really loved him, she would do what he suggests. Perhaps the young man needed to know that in putting temptation in her way, he may have been doing the devil's work for him. These examples are rather obvious, but there are more subtle concerns that serious disciples should recognize.

As a pastor, one of my major concerns has been the unity of believers in the church fellowship. Bearing in mind that the church is made up exclusively of sinners (albeit forgiven sinners in the process of sanctification!), endless opportunities exist for things to go wrong. Sadly, when church members disagree, potential is great for lasting damage to the name of Christ and the testimony of the church. For example, two believers may look at the gifts of the Spirit differently. This is perfectly understandable seeing that even Paul "looked through a glass darkly" and that Peter found things that Paul had written hard to understand. Now, if believers could accept those facts and work together to understand the other's point of view, it could be most beneficial for all concerned.

Unfortunately, one of the people in the disagreement may
have difficulty with such an approach and will see the issue
as "a matter of principle." Integrity is questioned; charges of
heresy come next; name-calling begins; people take sides;
blood pressures rise; tempers flare; and a schism results.
Somewhere along the line, the unity of believers in the bond
of peace was destroyed; and this was hardly the work of the
Spirit, even though He and His gifts were the subject of disagreement. Somebody, somewhere, possibly very well-
meaning, did the devil's work for him. I am convinced that
this is an issue all too often totally overlooked by disciples.
Yet even a casual reading of the Master's dealing with Peter,
when he put temptation in His way, should give us great
pause for thought. Keeping this in mind can make a vast
difference in the way disciples treat each other and those
who do not acknowledge the Lord.

Next in the Mark passage comes the issue of mindset.
Jesus told Peter that he did not "have in mind the things of
God, but the things of men" (8:33). It might be argued that
because Peter was a man, it was hardly surprising that he
was thinking like a man rather than thinking like God. But
apparently the argument is without merit because the Master
clearly expected Peter's thinking to be governed by what he
had discovered of God's mind. While there is no suggestion
here that disciples should ignore mankind's discoveries in
keeping with the divine mandate to rule over creation, the
Master *was* objecting to the kind of human thinking that rules
out divine involvement in human affairs. The latter is exactly
what Peter was doing. Protagorus, the ancient Greek philoso-
pher, said, "Man is the measure of all things." It is this kind of
attitude and all its modern mutations which disciples need to
guard against.

For example, the modern businessman is often under great
pressure to come up with the right numbers at the end of
each fiscal quarter. If things are not going well, he might be
encouraged to "cut corners" by passing off an inferior prod-
uct, or skimping on materials, or shortchanging the time
spent on the job. All in the name of productivity! This kind of
"encouragement" can be most compelling when exercised by

the big boss. The modern-day disciple is frequently faced with a choice between doing what is right by God's standards or succumbing to the generally accepted standards of business morality, which usually leave much to be desired.

I have a friend who had spent his working life in the used car business. He became a disciple of the Lord Jesus and promptly began to follow Him earnestly. One day he called me and said that he could no longer function as a disciple in that particular business setting and he was quitting. I knew that he had never done anything else and it might be hard for him to start a new career at that stage of his life. So I urged caution while at the same time commending him for recognizing that disciples must decide whether or not they will do things God's way or man's. As I knew some used car dealers who were also genuine disciples, I encouraged him to meet with them and see how it was possible to be honest *and* successful. He did so and today is still an effective disciple of Jesus Christ skillfully disguised as a used car salesman.

Another monumental issue was raised by the Master in the same context. He announced, "Whoever wants to save his life will lose it, but whoever loses his life for Me and for the Gospel will save it" (Mark 8:35). This issue is surely one of the most significant because it has to do with how to avoid a wasted life, a subject in which seemingly everyone would be interested. Yet some people much prefer to duck the issue.

The United Negro College Fund runs some excellent ads on television asking viewers to support young black Americans who otherwise might not be able to attend college. The final sentence of the ad always makes an impact on me: "A mind is a terrible thing to waste." That is undoubtedly true and I might add, "A life is an even more terrible thing to waste." Jesus Christ was impressing on His disciples that it is all too easy for human beings to become so concerned about their own lives that they hold them tightly to their bosoms and seek to preserve them by keeping them for themselves. Paul reports that Jesus Himself once said, "It is more blessed to give than to receive" (Acts 20:35). But this truth is not generally accepted because human selfishness insists that it is better to get than to give.

Ivan Boesky, who made a name for himself in a 1987 Wall Street scandal, told the graduating class of the University of California at Berkeley, "I think greed is healthy. You can be greedy and still feel good about yourself." Apparently he was not just grandstanding to the students when he said this, because reputedly when relaxing at home he proudly wears a T-shirt with the slogan: "He who owns the most when he dies, wins." Unfortunately the Boesky doctrine has many devotees in the United States, many of whom are apparently unaware or unconcerned that either Ivan or Jesus is right. The issue of life's purpose and life's goals is far too serious to be left to slogans on T-shirts, particularly when they flatly contradict the words of Scripture.

I am reminded of the story of a man who spent all his life climbing the rungs of the corporate ladder. In the process he jeopardized his family, his health, and his friends, but he felt it worthwhile because life for him was his business. One fine day he reached the top rung of the ladder only to discover it was leaning against the wrong building! Like many of his contemporaries, he had ducked the crucial issue Jesus Christ raised with His disciples.

The Master also took aim at the society in which Peter and his fellow disciples were going to live out their discipleship. He called it an "adulterous and sinful generation" (Mark 8:38). By "adulterous," He meant that the generation to which they belonged had become unfaithful to God. This unfaithfulness included not only rejection of His requirements for sexual morality but all types of disregard for and disobedience to the Lord and His directions for life. If the modern word for having in mind the things of men rather than the things of God is *humanism*, the modern word for "adulterous and sinful generation" is *secularism*. The conjunction of the two terms is quite common today even though what people mean by "secular humanism" varies greatly.

Modern-day disciples, like Peter and his friends, need to recognize that the society to which they belong is shot through with attitudes and philosophies in diametric opposition to those the Master taught. Of course, it is one thing to recognize this, but quite another to know what to do about it!

As a result, it is not uncommon to meet disciples who are trying to address the problem in totally different ways. This is certainly true in our church.

The public school system is a case in point. Feelings run so deep on this subject because *our* kids are involved. Everyone is agreed that the system certainly is not being run by believers or on Christian principles. Some think our schools should be, and won't stand for anything less; others think that because we live in a pluralistic society, we must be part of it. Accordingly, some have decided that they must remove their children from the influences to which they might be subjected in the public school system. Some have decided to start Christian schools, while others have come to the conclusion that the proper place for education is in the home. So they are home-schooling their kids. Still others are concerned about the loss of Christian influence in the public schools and have decided not only to stay in them but to take positions of leadership whenever possible. As a result we have church members who are serving on the parent-teacher associations and others who have been elected to their school boards. Without getting into a discussion of the rights or wrongs (or betters and bests) of these differing positions, it is encouraging to see that parents are taking seriously the well-being of their children.

So we have some disciples of Jesus Christ skillfully disguised as schoolteachers, another as president of the school board, and a number who are home-school teachers. But they all recognize the dangers of casually fitting into the lifestyles of a secularized society. To do that may be to identify inappropriately with a generation which has callously turned its back on what God has in mind.

Of course, the disciple is not free to live in hermetically sealed isolation either. It is the challenge of balancing out the conflicting aspects of living Christianly in a non-Christian world which makes being a disciple so thrilling and exciting—because there is no shortage of issues which disciples of Jesus confront. And the real ones don't duck or flinch. They meet the issues head on and keep on following.　　　　◆

e l e v e n

Refresher Course

A GOLDEN RULE in all communication is this: "If you want people to listen to you, talk about something they are interested in hearing." That makes sense, but it also poses problems. For example, "What are people interested in today?" All kinds of things, most of which begin with the letters s-e-l-f. If we accept that people are basically interested in themselves and how to feel good about themselves, those of us who try to communicate to them must talk about "self."

The word used in some quarters for this self-centeredness is *narcissism.* Narcissus was a rather tragic figure in Greek mythology. He was disappointed in love and one day, wandering disconsolately by a lake, he saw his reflection, and promptly fell in love with himself. Self-absorption is as equally disappointing as a failed romance. Nevertheless, it is extremely popular and prevalent. The result has been that many communicators nowadays have taken to talking to people about self-assertion and self-advancement. When these communicators happen to be preachers, however, they run into a massive problem: if people want to hear about themselves, how do you get them interested in God? The answer to that one has been to show people how God can help them in their self-whatever.

No doubt this is valid as far as it goes, but how do you avoid giving the impression that the main thing about God is that He can help you feel better about yourself? And how do you teach people that God in Christ said, "If anyone would come after Me, *he must deny himself* and take up his cross and follow Me"? (Mark 8:34, italics added)

I have noticed two faulty approaches to solving this dilemma. One is to ignore it altogether and never mention what Christ said about "denying self." The other is to initially present a message which concentrates on God as the One who assists us in our search for self, and then later introduce the less appealing aspects of what Christ taught. This second approach has two problems. The first is that people thus approached often feel as if they have been given an insurance policy which contains fine print they only discover after signing up. This tactic does not make them more receptive to Christ; on the contrary, it makes them feel duped. The second, and main problem, is that Christ Himself did not use this approach.

Christ did not teach the concept of self-denial to His disciples only after they had embarked on a life of following Him. Mark is careful to state that when He said these striking words "He called *the crowd* to Him along with His disciples" (8:34, italics added). Apparently He told people right from the beginning that the life that He was inviting them to share with Him was one which would challenge them to the core of their being. At the same time, He required His disciples to listen again to what they had presumably already heard. They needed a refresher course in what discipleship involves.

I am convinced that we need to bear these two things in mind. We must let people know what discipleship involves right from the beginning of our communication about Christ. And we must go on reminding each other of the challenge of being a follower of the Lord Jesus, because there are many aspects of discipleship that would be both easy and convenient to forget.

I am quite aware that believers hold differing opinions on this subject. Some say that we should invite people to simply trust Christ and later teach them about discipleship. Others insist that the only Christ they can be invited to trust is the *Lord* Christ and therefore "simply trusting" Him must also

include acknowledging His lordship. The former respond to
that suggestion with charges that "works" are being required
for redemption; the latter reply that you can't ask people to
trust Christ if you have not told them that He is the Lord.

At the risk of getting into trouble with both sides of the
debate, I suggest that we clearly cannot require *total* acknowledgment of Christ's lordship for salvation, because acknowledging His lordship is an ongoing experience. And who
of us would ever claim to continually and totally submit to
Him? On the other hand, those we invite in Christ's name to
follow Him need to be alerted to the challenge of what they
are getting into as well as the blessing they can anticipate.
Therefore, an adequate response to Christ should incorporate
a readiness to follow Him and a readiness to learn more and
more about the Christian life as we go along.

Now let's look carefully at what Jesus actually told the
crowd and the disciples in Mark 8:34. Notice there are four
responses that the Lord clearly expects from His disciples:
1. Come after Me.
  2. Deny yourself.
    3. Take up your cross.
      4. Follow Me.
We'll discuss the first of these responses for the remainder of
this chapter and the other three in chapter 12.

The phrase "come after" looks straightforward enough, but
it is worth noting that the expression was used to denote a
lover following the beloved, a servant following the master,
as well as a pupil following the teacher. On one occasion,
when I was preaching in Charlotte Chapel in Edinburgh, Scotland, a young lady gave her testimony before the sermon. She
was pretty, articulate, and vivacious—and obviously very
much in love. But her story was riveting even if she had had
none of the above going for her! She reminded the congregation that she was one of their missionaries serving as a nurse
in Kabul, Afghanistan during the Soviet aggression in that
country. Then she told how she had met a young man in
Afghanistan, that they had fallen in love, and he had asked
her to marry him. (By this time even the dour Scots were
looking a little sentimental!) She then blew my mind by ex-

plaining that she did not feel that she could answer the young man until she had talked to the elders of the church who had commissioned her to serve as a missionary. That was why she had flown home to seek their counsel.

As she sat down beside me after her talk, I thanked her for speaking in such a fashion and then I said jokingly to her, "Did you notice the young guy sitting on the front row? You really got his attention!"

"That's him," she responded.

"That's him? Who's him?"

"That's the young man who wants to marry me."

"But I thought he was in Afghanistan!"

"He was," she replied. "But when he heard I was flying back, he jumped on a plane and came too!"

As I looked at her shining face, I knew this was a disciple of Jesus Christ skillfully disguised as a woman in love.

For that young man to fly from Afghanistan to Scotland was a somewhat dramatic and expensive exercise. But everyone who has ever been in love knows what the young couple was feeling and would smile in approval. To *come after* her like this was the romantic action of a lover following his beloved.

There is a sense in which modern-day disciples need to discover this kind of loving recklessness and, having discovered it, to keep it fresh and alive. You may have noticed, as I have, that young believers often start out with a freshness in their love for Christ, but that freshness is not always maintained. We may attribute this to a maturing of love, rather similar to the more sensible and sedate love which couples share after thirty years of marriage as compared to the love of their honeymoon. This is a valid point, but I still think that it is all too common for believers to become less than excited about loving the Lord and increasingly mundane as a result. We need to continually *come after* Christ.

When I was a young boy during World War II, Captain H.S. May of the Royal Artillery became a frequent guest in my parents' home. He was stationed nearby and, being single, he enjoyed the fellowship which our home provided. But I doubt if he enjoyed it as much as I enjoyed him. To me, he was

fresh and vibrant, exciting, and well worth emulating. And I'm
not just talking about him being a military man. He was a
disciple of Jesus Christ skillfully disguised as a career soldier.
Though he must be ninety by now, he writes to me quite
often. And he is as refreshing in his discipleship today as he
has ever been. Why? Because after all these years he still
enjoys the Lord and loves Him unabashedly.

Wherever the President of the United States travels, he is
surrounded by an entourage. One man is never far from his
side. He carries a small case which contains the most sensi-
tive materials necessary for a President to have constantly
available in an age where nuclear holocaust is always a possibility. This man's dutiful, quiet, unobtrusive following of the
President is crucial. For our purposes, it also illustrates appropriate disciple behavior, coming after Christ in the same
way that a servant follows his master.

Percy Robinson was a small man whose diminutive stature
was accentuated by a severe curvature of the spine. His wife
had died, leaving him alone in a tiny home where he lived
quietly and frugally. By day he earned his living as a printer.
During my lunch hours, when I was a young banker, I would
often eat a sandwich with Percy among the ink and the press-
es, which looked as if they had been bought cheaply from a
print shop in Charles Dickens' time. He talked always about
serving the Lord. He delivered his printing on time at rates
which were so low that he barely eked out a living. When I
asked Percy about this, he said he didn't want to abuse people. He was unobtrusive, even to the point of being regarded
as something of a village eccentric. But when Percy died, a
brash businessman who was not known for handing out ac-
colades said, "If ever there was a Christian it was Percy the
Printer." Obviously another skillfully disguised disciple of
Jesus Christ.   ◆

More Refreshing

DENYING OURSELVES generally is not one of our favorite pastimes. However, I must admit that in recent years the "self" movement has helped us focus in on physical fitness, making us very diet- and exercise-conscious. This has been most beneficial for many people, myself included! Eating less and better, getting out of bed and sweating rather than staying in bed and vegetating, has required a certain degree of self-denial which is commendable in a society which has become increasingly self-indulgent.

We must also acknowledge that self-denial is something that many people engage in once a year for religious reasons. It is unfortunate that the denying of self which the Master talked about has been confused with the self-denial of periodic Lenten observance or the means to achieving the end of a better figure and a healthier life, as good as these things are.

The Master was addressing something much deeper than any or all of these concerns. He was pointing out that men and women need to recognize that their lives can be dominated by their own self-interests, or they can be subjected to the interests and concerns of the One who created and redeemed them. To submit to the interests of the Creator-Saviour automatically requires the denying of self-centered interests that would militate against His desires and plans. So a decision has to be made. Who is going to be in charge?

At the end of World War II, the Conservative Party, led by Winston Churchill, was challenged in a general election by the Labor Party, led by Clement Attlee. Churchill, who had been immensely popular during the war years, was now being portrayed by his opponents as a "warmonger." And since the British people had had enough war to last them a number of lifetimes, some began to question whether they wanted Churchill as a peacetime leader who might get them into another war. One day a leading newspaper ran a cartoon which depicted a revolver held in a hand with a finger on the trigger. The caption read simply, "Whose finger on the trigger?" Many political analysts say that the cartoon probably contributed more than anything else to Churchill's rejection by the British people after the war.

I have never been able to forget the question, "Whose finger on the trigger?" not just because of its political implications for all generations, but also because of its moral and spiritual implications for all who are faced with the choice of who will be the dominant power in their lives.

Deciding to respond to the challenge and invitation to be a disciple is not unlike responding to the challenge and invitation to be married. There is a sense in which all kinds of preparations for marriage can be made. (I'm not talking about the preparations for the wedding, which often supersede adequate preparations for marriage. This has always bothered me, seeing that the wedding lasts a half hour and the marriage is supposed to last a lifetime!) Indeed, those who contemplate marriage should have some idea of the nature of the commitment they are about to make. But there is no doubt that the old Englishman was right when he said concerning marriage, "You never know what you've got until you get them home and the door's shut!" Therefore, the best a man or woman can do is to have a good idea in principle about what marriage is really about, realizing the practicalities can only be known once the agreement has been made and the new relationship begun.

In the same way, the Master clearly talked about denying self as a factor in discipleship. Those who entered into a relationship with Jesus presumably did so with at least a modicum of understanding that changes would be necessary in their lives, because they would be learning to say no to self-interest when it conflicted with the Master's interests. But having made the first step, they needed to be frequently reminded of their commitment to start working it out in practice. In the same way that marriage only works as the promises and commitments of the wedding day are applied on a continual basis, so the realities of discipleship require an ongoing willingness to deny self as the day-to-day challenges arise.

For example, I may be addicted to Monday Night Football, but I know that my church needs sponsors for the boys' club on Monday nights and I have a nasty, gnawing feeling that I should be helping. What do I do? Well, I could try to rationalize my situation and say that I always have a hard day on Mondays, and I need to relax, and God knows this so He wouldn't want me overextending myself. Or I could say, "Who am I kidding? I'm not all that tired and I really should be helping with those kids. And come to think of it, I can probably be back in time for the second half of the game anyway!" Giving up half of a football game may not sound like a big piece of denying self to many people (particularly women!), but I can assure you that it would be a monumental step forward for a number of men I know who haven't really begun to work through the hard-nosed realities of denying themselves as an integral part of discipleship.

We are so familiar with the expression "take up his cross" that we might not be able to realize the shock with which Christ's words must have been received. Crucifixion was a Roman, as opposed to Jewish, means of capital punishment. In fact, only the Romans could exercise the death penalty in the days when Christ was living in Israel; and Jewish law reserved a special curse for anyone hanged on a tree (see Deut. 21:23). We have no way of knowing how much the crowd and the disciples grasped when the Master spoke these words, but they must have had some idea, for they were all familiar with the dreadful sight of condemned criminals wending their way to the place of crucifixion carrying the cross-beam of the cross on which they would soon die.

For centuries the cross has been a stark symbol of the Christian faith and rightly so, for it points to the central and unique event—namely, the Master's death and resurrection—without which our faith would be invalid. It appears on steeples and Communion tables, letterheads and necklaces, even baseball hats and T-shirts; and as it does, it speaks of Christ, however feebly or powerfully. But as important as symbols undoubtedly are to our faith, we cannot afford to relegate the idea of the disciple's cross bearing either to cross wearing or to church decorating.

The Master was talking about an attitude of heart which would so identify His disciples with Him and His cause that if it led them to pain and suffering, loss and even death, they would carry through His desires and be found faithful to the end.

I have known friends who in the depth of their depression and emotional imbalance have wished to die and have precipitated their own demise. But I know of no red-blooded, normal person who wishes to die and goes about seeking ways to accomplish his or her wishes. The Master was not looking for emotionally unstable people who were suffering from a morbid death wish. He was looking for people who would be normal and healthy and courageous enough to stand firm in His name if and when the time came to stand up and be counted for their association with Him. I don't believe that anyone knows in advance how he or she will react to mortal danger, but I do believe that it is possible to be so resolute in Christ that one can be willing to take up the cross if and when called upon to do so.

I will never forget spending time with young black church leaders from the township of Soweto near Johannesburg, South Africa. They told me about the extreme pressures they were working under as they endeavored to minister faithfully in the name of Christ to many desperately needy people. The political situation was—and still is—extremely volatile and they said they felt trapped between powerful forces. On the one hand, the Marxists were making thinly disguised overtures to them to be involved in their push for "liberation." On the other hand, government agents were watching them closely to see if they participated at all with the Marxists. These believers told me that they were committed only to the Lord Jesus and His church, and wished only to see righteousness and justice prevail. But they added somberly that if violence did eventually break out (and they expected it would), that they would be caught in between, trusted by neither force, treated with reserve by blacks and whites, and possibly their lives would be forfeit. All this they spoke without a note of self-pity. In fact, there was a calmness about them that served only to remind me that in our generation, bearing the cross has meant intense pain and suffering and even death to vast numbers of disciples.

But what about those of us who live in much more agreeable and benign circumstances? Are we exempt from cross bearing? I think not. There is a sense in which suffering comes for all who would follow Christ. Sometimes people tell me about their terrible marriages and then with great courage say, "Well, I guess it's my cross and I'll just have to bear it." At the risk of appearing insensitive to their dilemma, however, I try to tell them gently that bearing the cross is not putting a brave face on the inevitable. When Jesus took up His cross, that certainly was not the case. Neither is taking up the cross putting up with the consequences of our own bad decisions. Taking up the cross means so committing ourselves to the Master's will for our lives that, as life unfolds one day at a time, we might be found faithfully carrying our burdens even through pain and suffering and, in some relatively rare occasions, death itself.

We have already said much about following Christ, but one further thought might help. The Master laid great stress on the need for perseverance in the life of following. He once said, "He who stands firm to the end will be saved" (Matt. 24:13), and this is a needed emphasis for our day. We live at a time when "short term" has become fashionable. Young people go to college and switch majors and juggle courses to see what they like and don't like. They graduate and get jobs which they keep as long as they want to—until a more attractive offer is made (management, of course, is equally fickle). They move from one neighborhood to another and switch from city to city all in the name of upward mobility. Houses and cars, churches and friends suffer the transient treatment, so it is no surprise that marriages and families too are traded in when convenient. The result is a rootless and shallow society. People of this "short term" generation have been heard to say that they will "give Christianity a try to see if they like it." That is certainly better than them not trying Christianity at all, but it is a long way from the following that perseveres to the end.

In 1555, the gifted English Reformers Hugh Latimer and Nicholas Ridley were taken to Oxford where they were required to defend their theological position and their commitment to Christ. What they had to say was rejected and they were sentenced to be burned at the stake. This death was unusually slow and excruciatingly painful because burning materials in England have always been damp. As the two men stood helpless, choking in the acrid fumes, Latimer said to his friend, "Be of good comfort, Master Ridley, and play the man. We shall this day light such a candle by God's grace in England as I trust shall never be put out." That's one way of illustrating what it means to keep on following.

Remember that many have embarked on a life of Christian profession only to fade from view when adversity reared its ugly head. Disciples of Jesus keep on keeping on—even to the end. ◆

I Didn't Promise You a Rose Garden

LIFE IS A WONDERFUL learning experience! This is because we learn in different ways and at different levels. It is one thing to sit on the edge of a pool and read a book about swimming techniques. It is another thing entirely to be pushed off the deep end and be called upon to sink or swim! The former approach suffers from being somewhat academic and superficial; the latter is much more practical and effective, assuming the learner survives the experience.

Life puts us in all kinds of situations from which we learn great truths. But if the truth were known, we would never have learned them at all; because if it were left up to us, we would have avoided the learning experience. Which person who cannot swim volunteers to be pushed off the deep end?

It is important to note that a major part of the Twelve's discipling-learning process was experience related. Certainly there were times when they sat at Christ's feet and learned the Word from Him, but it was in the hustle and bustle of working among the people that they grew. It was as they faced the challenge of applying what Jesus had told them to the harsh situations of life that they began to discover the truth about their own abilities, or lack of them, and the superb resources available through their relationship to the Master. Life is not lived in a vacuum and disciples aren't made in a classroom.

With this in mind, the Lord "called the Twelve together . . .
and sent them out to preach the kingdom of God and to heal
the sick" (Luke 9:1-2). Up until this point, they had played a
minor role in His ministry, but He had been close at hand to
help them out if they got into difficulties. Now, however, they
were being "sent out." They were about to experience what
every learner pilot has had to face: the awful thought of flying
solo, without the instructor's hands on the controls!

The ministry the disciples were given was twofold. They
were "to preach the kingdom of God *and* to heal the sick."
Theirs was simply an extension of the ministry that Christ
Himself had been engaged in. But now they were being called
upon to be the means of His reaching out beyond the limitations of His own assumed humanity. Like the rest of us, Jesus
only had one pair of hands and could only be in one place at
a time. Twelve more pairs of hands would go a long way
toward reaching out to the multitudes for whom He had
shown such compassion.

On the occasion of healing a blind man, the Master had
asserted forcefully, "While I am in the world, I am the light of
the world" (John 9:5). But during the Sermon on the Mount,
He had told the disciples "You are the light of the world"
(Matt. 5:14). He was already letting them know that the day
would come when He would no longer be present in the
world in the way that He was at that particular time, and that
when that day came, their task would be to continue what He
had started. Now they were about to embark on the first
shaky steps towards achieving that end. The significance for
us modern disciples is that we are the extension of all that He
initiated and they perpetuated.

The effectiveness of ministry today is often measured by
sophisticated means which rely heavily on statistics and all
kinds of state-of-the-art anthropological and sociological
measurements which may or may not be helpful. But there
should be no doubt that we can always measure the effectiveness of how we are doing spiritually against the yardstick of
our goal: to be what Christ was and do what He did, as
illustrated for us by those early disciples.

The balance of His (and their) ministry was clear—they

were first and foremost concerned about the spiritual and physical needs of people. The church's mission today is no different. But having said that, we still have to discern the relational priority between spiritual and physical needs. Should we deal with physical needs as a means of getting to the spiritual needs? For instance, if a country is closed to Christian missions, should we go in as medical personnel so that we can quietly preach the kingdom to the people? Or should meeting physical needs be seen as an integral part of our mission of grace and mercy—so that even if we can't witness verbally, we still recognize the intrinsic worth of helping hurting people in the name of Christ?

Or, on the other side of the coin, should we regard physical ministry as a natural outcome of spiritual ministry? In other words, only if we see people become disciples would we then have a responsibility to meet their physical needs? Different segments of the body of Christ have arrived at different answers to these questions at different stages of church history, and, accordingly, different emphases of ministry have developed. But whatever the relative merits of either approach to ministry we embrace, it should be obvious that some balance of the two is necessary if the work of the kingdom is to be continued.

When I was a high school student, the headmaster once asked for a volunteer who could drive a horse and cart to transport some equipment from the school to an area sports ground, in preparation for the annual school athletic day. The thought of a day out of school appealed to me immensely, so I volunteered—although I had never driven a horse and cart in my life. I can still remember the mingled feelings of pride and terror when I took the reins and embarked on what turned out to be a disastrous experience. The outward journey went by without a hitch, but as we were unloading the equipment, a donkey—which had gotten free from somewhere—went by, spooked my horse, and off it took. There was no way I could catch the horse and I waited until someone eventually stopped its mad race, and brought it and what was left of the cart and equipment back to me! Was my face ever red when I got back to school!

My problem was that I had been given authority to drive the horse, but I did not have the corresponding power to handle the authority. Now, of course, someone else who had the power to drive it could have taken the horse and driven it away, but he would have done so without the headmaster's authority. So you see, power without authority may be effective but illegitimate, while authority without power is legitimate but ineffective. That is why the Master's action in sending out the disciples is so important. "He gave them *power and authority* to drive out all demons and to cure diseases" (Luke 9:1, italics added).

The disciples were no strangers to the powerful forces of the spiritual world, for they had seen people suffering from all manner of disabilities, and they had observed firsthand the conflict in which the Master had been engaged when He had challenged the realms of spiritual darkness. So while they were not totally ignorant of what they were getting into, it is doubtful if they fully understood the extent of the fight between the kingdom of Satan and the kingdom of God. They would soon find out, of course!

The same can be said for the modern disciple who has watched from the sidelines the struggle between those who stand firmly for the things of God against those who propagate the things of the Evil One. Only those who have endeavored to move into enemy-held territory have any idea of the stress and strain involved, and, accordingly, they are the only ones who begin to discover the resources of authority and power with which disciples have been invested.

In our church we have a number of people who have shown great concern about the proliferation of pornography in their neighborhoods. They have become organized, acquainted themselves with state legislation, and addressed those who are selling pornography, pointing out especially the harmful effects on children who go into convenience stores where such material is publicly displayed. In a number of instances, the response has been most favorable and pornography has been removed from the shelves. But in others, these crusading men and women have found themselves in a battle. Such, however, is the lot of the disciple in any era—

and that is why the sense of power and authority is so significant.

If the disciples of Jesus had any doubts about the reality of spiritual warfare, those doubts vanished when the Master said (in a slightly different context), "Go! I am sending you out like lambs among wolves" (Luke 10:3). Disciples need to be reminded of these words for two reasons. First, if they have any degree of success, they may forget they are lambs and try to roar like lions; second, if they forget they are up against wolves, they may think they are engaged in a picnic. Only disaster can result from assuming that lambs snarl and wolves bleat, in the same way that it is fatal if military strategists overestimate their own strengths and underestimate those of the enemy.

As if to underline the seriousness and urgency of the disciples' mission, the Master instructed them, "Take nothing for your journey—no staff, no bag, no bread, no money, no extra tunic" (Luke 9:3). That's what you call traveling light! In trying to understand the reason for this prohibition, we should remember that on a later occasion Jesus reminded them of this experience and asked them specifically if they had lacked anything. When they testified that they had been well cared for, He then told them to take along a purse and a bag and even a sword! (Luke 22:35-36) So apparently Christ had in mind that they should learn a lesson in trusting as they stepped out on risk's edge, and He was clearly not making an absolute prohibition for all disciples for all time.

It is also interesting to note that the limitations Jesus placed on the disciples' equipment were very similar to the rabbinic restrictions placed on men entering the temple to worship—the idea behind the rabbis' code being that when men came to worship they should leave other concerns behind and concentrate on what they were supposed to do. Thus it is legitimate for us to interpret Jesus' instructions as a reminder to the disciples that they should be wholly committed to their task and should rid themselves of possible hindrances to its completion. Modern disciples need to be constantly reminded of this, because of the tensions that always exist to live by kingdom standards in a society which regards such standards either as irrelevant or unacceptable.

The Lord warned the disciples to expect two possible reactions to their ministries. There would be those who would welcome them to stay in their homes, and the disciples should take care not to abuse the kindness of these people. Then there would be those who would have nothing to do with them. In that case, they were told, "Shake the dust off your feet when you leave their town, as a testimony against them" (Luke 9:5). It was customary for orthodox Jews to carefully remove dust from their sandals after passing through Gentile territory. So by publicly removing the dust from their feet, the disciples would be telling the inhospitable and unresponsive among their fellow man that their rejection of the message of the kingdom put them in the same category as Gentiles who were strangers to the covenant God had made with His people. This was hardly designed to gain the disciples many friends, but to show the people the seriousness of their rejection.

As they set off on their adventure, the disciples were embarking not only on a mission but also on an experience, where they would learn tremendous lessons about spiritual conflict, power and authority as delegated by God to human beings, urgency, single-mindedness, trust, and faithfulness. There never was a disciple who, having come out of his shell and embarked on a life of ministry, did not learn the selfsame lessons and grow immeasurably as a result.

When I was teaching in a Bible school in England, I was concerned about the excessive time the young people were spending at their desks, and thought it would be good if we could get them out into the cold world for some practical application of what they had been learning. So I checked with some friends in a nearby city and asked if they had any jobs in their churches which nobody wanted to do. Not surprisingly, they had lots of jobs which fell into that category. Arrangements were made for our students to do the jobs in return for a roof over their heads, some food in their stomachs, and a place to sleep. Then I went to the students and told them about our upcoming adventure. Immediately, we had a very strange epidemic—everyone got sick.

One husky young man came to me and said, "I can't go."
"Why not?" I asked.
"Because I've lost my voice," he replied huskily.
"Why should that stop you from going?"
"I can't communicate," he replied even more huskily.
"You just communicated to me despite the fact that you've lost your voice, so you shouldn't have any problems." Then I added, to my own surprise, "Anyway, you haven't lost your voice. You're just chicken!"
"No," he insisted with even less voice. "No, I've lost my voice."
"Let me tell you something. You're chicken; I'm chicken; everybody's chicken around here!"
He looked stunned for a moment, and then said with a fully recovered voice, "You're not!"
That was the day I discovered two spiritual gifts that I didn't know I possessed: discernment and healing!
The result was that we loaded our bunch of chickens on buses and traveled to the tough areas of that industrial city; and with hearts beating their way out of our chests, we had a great time. Never were the students more alert to their studies. Never were they more anxious to pray, and never were they more excited about being disciples. So you see, disciples of Jesus Christ are sometimes skillfully disguised as chickens! ◆

Learning by Making Mistakes

PEGGY KIRK BELL was one of the first professional women golfers. She is also a master teacher of the Ladies' Professional Golf Association and a close friend of our family. We have visited her beautiful golf resort in North Carolina for vacations and conferences on a number of occasions, and each time she takes me to the practice tee and gives me a lesson. I enjoy golf, but I am still inclined to think it is a good walk spoiled. Nevertheless, I always appreciate the chance to learn from Peggy, who once suggested to me that the only thing I needed to do to correct my golf game was to pick up a club between annual lessons!

Peggy's teaching approach is quite simple. She gives you a bucket of a few hundred balls and lets you swing at them. The result, for me at least, is that I send turf further than the ball at first. So Peggy shows me why I'm hitting behind the ball and corrects it. Then I start to hit the ball—but not very far. Peggy shows me why I'm topping the ball and makes the necessary adjustment. Then the ball starts to fly, but unfortunately it goes in a great slicing arc over the trees. I make a couple additional adjustments to my swing, and eventually the ball begins to go more or less where it is intended. In fact, I suspect that if I could dispense with half my clubs and put Peggy in my golf bag, I'd probably be on the pro tour! But note her method. She lets you swing away and make your mistakes so that they are obvious to you and everybody else, and *then* she makes the corrections. It is called learning by making mistakes.

This was certainly one of the teaching-discipling methods which the Master, our Lord Jesus, used. But such a philosophy has never been overly popular with His followers. One reason for this is undoubtedly the common fear of failure. We are so success oriented that anything less than "winning" is regarded as unacceptable and to be avoided at all costs. One of the easiest ways of avoiding defeat is to refuse to enter the contest and this is exactly what happens for some disciples. Rather than risk looking foolish or feeling inadequate, they prefer to stick with the tested and tried things they can handle with ease, thus never launching out into new areas of endeavor and discovery.

Then, there is the idea that only excellence will do for the Master, which, while commendable in its intent, is decidely debilitating in its outworking. Who will try anything new if they know that only excellence is acceptable? And how is excellence achieved if people aren't encouraged to learn, if necessary, by making mistakes?

I remember a conversation with Dave, my elder son, when he was a little boy. We were discussing things we should pray about and he couldn't think of anything. (He was more interested in going to sleep at the time!) I suggested a few possibilities, but he didn't seem impressed by any of them; so I asked him about school and if perhaps he might be having a hard time with any of the other kids. He looked surprised and asked me why I would wonder about that.

"Well, sometimes kids give other kids a hard time if they know they are Christians," I explained.

"Oh," he responded without any evident interest.

"Well, do they give *you* a hard time because you're a Christian?"

"No."

"Why do you think that is?" I queried.

"Probably because they don't know I am a Christian," Dave replied with great candor.

"Don't you think you should let them know?"

"No, I don't. If they give you a hard time, it's better not to tell them!" With that, he rolled over in his bed and slept like a baby!

In all fairness to Dave, who is now in the ministry, I must remind you that he was a young boy at the time, and his father was not using much common sense in pursuing the conversation either! But while Dave's approach was perfectly understandable for a small boy, it is hardly acceptable for those who profess to be disciples yet are paralyzed in their walk with the Master for fear of failure or trauma. Making mistakes is part of life in general and being a disciple in particular. Mistakes are inevitable, but if handled wisely they can be immensely valuable. Moreover, the old proverb is true: "He who never made a mistake never made anything."

Illustrations abound of Jesus' teaching through allowing mistakes to be made, and the disciples' learning through making mistakes. For instance, "He took Peter, John, and James with Him and went up onto a mountain to pray" (Luke 9:28). Christ was anxious to pray because He was getting closer to the consummation of His mission on planet earth. Thus it was necessary for Him to reaffirm His commitment to bearing His own cross, and to draw afresh from the Father the resources necessary for the task. Apparently, He desired the supportive presence of the inner circle of disciples, but He was not to get it. Oh, they went along all right, but they found (as many later disciples have discovered) that all-night prayer meetings are hard work—and they fell asleep on the job.

When Peter, James, and John awakened, they were utterly astonished to see that the Master was talking to Moses and Elijah, and that all three "appeared in glorious splendor" (v. 31). These three disciples were spectators of the most dramatic show of divine beauty imaginable, so it is hardly surprising that Peter blurted out, "Let us put up three shelters—one for You, one for Moses, and one for Elijah" (v. 33). Presumably he wanted to perpetuate the glory of the moment, but two things should be noted. First, his suggestion was ignored, and second, Luke in his gospel adds the terse comment, "He did not know what he was saying." In other words he had opened his mouth once again and put his foot in it!

It is a perfectly human and normal desire to want to extend a pleasant experience. So no one can really criticize Peter's desire, but the problem was that he was unwittingly getting in the way of the cross again. He wanted the mountaintop and not the valley. He much preferred the glory to the shame. And who of us would not have taken exactly the same route? His mistake was born of ignorance and excessive enthusiasm.

Thankfully, ignorance can be cured and excessive enthusiasm can be tempered. And when these exercises are completed, the result is a much more mature person. But both exercises take time.

A preacher once announced that he was going to speak on the topic, "Ignorance and Apathy."

"What's ignorance and apathy?" a man leaned over and asked his wife.

"I don't know and I don't care!" she replied.

Nobody could accuse Peter of ignorance and apathy, but he did have problems with ignorance and enthusiasm. Apathy will never cause waves (or anything else). On the other hand, enthusiasm can always be counted on to achieve something—but not always something desirable.

Recently I came across the notes of my first sermon preached when I was seventeen years old. It was a humbling experience to say the least, but it was also encouraging. Humbling, because I saw quickly how much I didn't know at the time, but encouraging, because it reminded me of the opportunities I was given as a young teenager to develop that aspect of my discipleship. There was ignorance in abundance but there was no lack of enthusiasm, and over the years I have had wonderful people around me who have helped me work on my monumental ignorance without destroying my enthusiasm.

The day after the remarkable events on the mountain, the disciples of Jesus were busy making some mistakes. They had encountered a man desperately seeking healing for his demon-possessed son. With great enthusiasm, they had responded to the father's request, only to discover that they were up against a particularly tough kind of demon that showed no respect whatsoever for them or their attempts at exorcism.

Imagine the scene as crowds gathered around the boy who lay writhing on the ground, foaming at the mouth, while the disciples tried desperately to deal with the situation. We have to give the Twelve credit for trying. Most disciples would have headed for the bushes in a similar situation today. No, there was nothing wrong with their enthusiasm at this point; but they *had* forgotten that their warfare was spiritual, and, therefore, they were failing to use the proper spiritual weapons of prayer and faith (see Mark 9:28-29). Despite all their efforts and warmhearted response to the pitiful boy, they came up short by a mile. This was frustrating and humiliating, but not to them only.

At this point, the Master stepped in. He was obviously frustrated with their mistaken approach to the problem and He castigated them for being part of an "unbelieving and perverse generation" (Luke 9:41). It has often been said that "a little knowledge is a dangerous thing," and the same can be said for a little success. Given the success of their previous mission, the disciples had presumably bought into the idea that they now had the answers and the ability to do the job and all it required was hard work, enthusiasm, and know-how. This is a mistake that disciples through the years have repeated with monotonous regularity. But how were they and how are we to learn this lesson without moving rashly into situations and stubbing our evangelical toes? Ideally, we can all remember the lessons and avoid the mistakes. Yet given the human propensity for stupidity, we must accept the possibility that we will continue making mistakes. Let's just hope we will learn the lessons while doing only minimum damage.

Peter was not the only culprit when it came to making mistakes. James and John were equally capable! One day John came across a man driving out demons, but whose credentials, in John's opinion, were not acceptable. So John forbid the man to continue, then reported his "good deed" to the Master. To his chagrin, instead of being commended for his vigilance and enthusiastic rooting out of error, the Lord scolded, "Do not stop him, for whoever is not against you is

for you" (Luke 9:50). A similar event took place soon afterward. John and James went into a Samaritan village looking
for lodging and food for the disciples, but were not made
welcome. (The Samaritans took a poor view of people passing through their real estate on the way to the temple in
Jerusalem, because they thought Mount Gerizim was the
proper place to worship.) This did not sit well with the brothers, so they asked Jesus for permission to "call fire down
from heaven to destroy them" (v. 54). John and James were
presumably aware that this sort of thing happened when Elijah was around, and they thought it would be an appropriate
response to the rejection of their beloved Master by the ob-
durate Samaritans. Again the Lord rebuked the disciples for
their attitude. Note that on both these occasions there was no
shortage of enthusiasm, but tolerance was in decidedly short
supply.

Bad mistakes are common when disciples are called upon
to deal with differences of understanding and practice. Whenever the Master's people are vigilant for truth and opposed to
error, they are to be commended. But when their enthusiastic
countering of perceived error leads them to speak authorita-
tively where Scripture preserves a reverent silence, or where
their legitimate actions are so strong as to destroy the people
concerned, then mistakes are made and corrections are in
order. Let's just remember that learning is supposed to take
place through the corrective measures.

Recently I was talking to the wife of a professional athlete.
The coach he played for previously had left the ball club, and
a new coach had been appointed. As a result, the athlete's
play had improved so dramatically that he was the talk of the
league. The wife was naturally delighted because he had not
always been treated well by the fans. When I asked what had
made the difference, she said, "One obvious reason is that the
style of play has changed under the new coach; and they are
playing more to his strengths, so he has the chance to shine.
But the main reason is that if he made a mistake under the
previous coach, he was promptly benched. But under the new
coach, he is allowed to make a mistake or two, and this gives
him time to settle down and play his game."

To me, one of the most endearing things about the Master's handling of His disciples was His willingness to teach them through the mistakes they made. He could quite easily have benched them all. Or perhaps He might simply have placed them on waivers! But fortunately, this has never been His method—not then, not now. This is an encouragement to all disciples who have failed and been devastated by their failure, or even for disciples who have never failed for the simple reason they have never tried. The good news is that Jesus Christ has many disciples skillfully disguised as failures. ♦

Who Is the Greatest?

IT IS UNFORTUNATE that we have burdened Christ's first disciples with the kind of sainthood that places them on marble pedestals at least six feet above contradiction. The result has been that we look at them through rose-tinted spectacles, which Scripture insists we have no right to wear. True, the Twelve had been set apart by God, and in this sense were saints; but in the more commonly accepted sense of the word, these men were no saints—and neither are we!

Perhaps we attempt to idealize the disciples because we like to think that they were so different from us that we don't need to emulate their example. If we can persuade ourselves that they were extraordinary, then we can explain their extraordinary success in terms of their extraordinary abilities. But if we accept that they were not at all extraordinary, we must explain their success some other way. And that explanation points unerringly to the fact that they were ordinary men who did extraordinary things because of their relationship with an extraordinary Master. If that is true, then we today are faced with a challenge of immense proportions: namely, being as ordinary as they were, we should expect to see the extraordinary done in us and through us because of a similar relationship to the identical extraordinary Master.

The disciples' ordinariness never came through more clearly than when they got into an argument about their pecking order. When our three children were young—I would guess ages two, four, and six—the two older ones marched the youngest into the room and said to Jill and me, "You're just going to have to do something about Peter!"

"Why, what on earth has he done now?" we inquired.

"It's not what he's done. It's what he thinks," they replied with great shows of righteous indignation.

"Well, what does he think that needs our attention?"

"He thinks he's as important as we are!"

"But he *is* as important as you are," we answered.

"Oh no, he isn't," said David. "He can't be, 'cause I'm number one."

"And I'm number two," chimed in Judy.

"So that makes him number three, and that's not as important as number one or number two!" they together shouted triumphantly.

I suppose at the ripe old ages of two, four, and six this kind of behavior is amusing. But in grown men, it is disconcerting, to say the least. But it happens all through life.

A friend of mine, an executive officer of a major league baseball team (not the Milwaukee Brewers!), told me about signing a new superstar for the club. As soon as the deal was announced, one of the team's current superstars, burst into the executive's office and shouted, "I don't know how much you're paying this blankety blank, but I demand a dollar a year more!" This from a multimillionaire who was having a hard time figuring out what to do with his money as it was. He clearly wasn't worried about another dollar. It was a matter of status, or to be more to the point, pride! And that was exactly the disciples' problem too.

Apart from demonstrating conclusively that the disciples still had little or no idea of the Master's intentions—because they were still thinking about an earthly kingdom and jockeying for position in it—the argument about who would be the greatest also shows that they had even less idea about what constitutes greatness. This, despite the fact that all of them had been told that denying self was an integral part of being a disciple. Here were some big egos that needed attention!

Taking a young child from the crowd, Jesus stood him

beside the disciples and said, "Whoever welcomes this little child in My name welcomes Me; and whoever welcomes Me welcomes the One who sent Me. For he who is least among you all—he is the greatest" (Luke 9:48).

People pushing for the top rarely notice those on the bottom of the pile. In fact, some people in their mad race for fame and fortune notice the "little people" only when they need them, and then do not hesitate to use them until their usefulness is spent. Politics gives us many examples of this kind of behavior. Many a politician in search of votes has become an ardent supporter of the underprivileged—until he is elected. Then he does little to alleviate their suffering; indeed, he even appears to forget the poor exist.

The thrust of Christ's words is this: whenever somebody is so committed to improving his own station in life that he stops caring for others—or worse, uses others to achieve his objectives—that person may achieve considerable fame, station, and celebrity in a secular environment, but rates very low in kingdom coinage. On the other hand, the person who has time for the little one in the name of Christ, and will even sacrifice self-interest on behalf of that little one, shows character well pleasing to the Master. That person is great in His eyes.

I have had the honor of working with many men and women who are well known in Christian circles. Many of them have been the most wonderful examples to me of genuine greatness. On my very first preaching tour of the U.S.A. as a young Britisher, I was quite nervous about the whole idea. When I discovered that the first week I would be sharing the ministry with Dr. Paul Rees, whom I had greatly admired for many years, my nervousness disappeared immediately and was superseded by total fright. But I need not have worried. Dr. Rees treated me as if I were the most capable preacher he had ever listened to. He sat on the front row taking notes as I preached; he came and asked me questions after I was through; and when he talked to me, he acted as if I were the only person on the planet. To my embarrassment, he also introduced me to everybody as "my dear friend, Stuart." The amazing thing to me was that it was all genuine. Greatness is not necessarily being well known. Greatness is a well-known man who in the name of Christ receives an unknown youngster starting out in ministry, makes him feel welcome, affirms him, and does all that he can to encourage him.

In Mark's account of the "Who is the greatest?" incident, another emphasis is brought out. Jesus said, "If anyone wants to be first, he must be the very last, and the servant of all" (9:35). One of the reasons people would like to be great is because they assume they can then call all the shots and have somebody else do the dirty work. But the Master's approach was totally different. Now we recognize, with the benefit of 20/20 hindsight, that He was looking toward His cross all the time He talked about serving and denying. But we should not overlook the wonderful way He demonstrated this same attitude in His life. When the wine ran out at the wedding feast, He served them with more. When the crowds were left hungry on the hillside, He banished their hunger pangs. When feet needed washing, He did the work.

But despite the Lord's teaching through both precept and illustration, the disciples were reluctant to commit themselves to that kind of lifestyle. Perhaps they had worked hard and long all their lives, and now they were looking for a more comfortable situation in the kingdom Jesus kept talking about, and in which they figured on being prominent members entitled to their share of perks.

Servanthood is regarded with amusement at best and outright rejection at worst in today's highly competitive world. For example, J. Paul Getty, one of the world's richest men, once said cynically, "The meek may inherit the earth—but not the mineral rights." And, of course, when it comes to the hard-nosed business of making a lot of money in oil, as he had done, he may well have been right. But there is an implied suggestion in his comment that something about owning mineral rights is far superior to anything the Master had to say about life both here and hereafter.

In marked contrast to the oil barons, Mother Teresa, the diminutive nun who has devoted herself to aiding some of the most desperately needy people on the face of the globe, has gained worldwide renown and practically universal affirmation by the simple, costly expedient of sacrificial service.

But the J. Paul Gettys and the Mother Teresas of this world are extreme examples, and we may have difficulty relating to them. The real question that needs addressing is: "What is it about receiving the little people and serving instead of being served that is so great?"

First, to be open to everyone shows that we have a proper perspective of our own and everyone's value as persons. This perspective is not gained through evaluation of commonly accepted status symbols, or through careful calculation of the relative benefits that accrue should one make the right connections and be seen in the right places with the right people. But, rather, it comes from an acceptance of the fundamental spiritual truths that we are all created by God, that all have sinned before God, and all are redeemable by God and have the potential to live eternally with Him.

Second, to be open to the possibility of serving rather than being served takes great humility. But true humility is not too hard to come by if we believe that we are, at worst, sinners and, at best, forgiven sinners. Winston Churchill surprised everyone by saying of his archrival Clement Attlee, "Mr. Attlee is a very humble man." But Churchill then added with typical scathing humor, "But of course he has a lot to be humble about!" No doubt he had a lot to be humble about because in the eyes of God we all have a lot to be humble about. To bear this in mind constantly is to be on the right road to developing a genuinely meek and humble spirit.

It is unfortunate that meekness and weakness sound so similar, because many people have assumed they are similar. But as Earl Radmacher once said, "If you think meekness is weakness, try being meek for a week!" In fact, it takes considerable strength to go about your life humbly before the Master, seeking to serve other people. Why? For the simple reason that the world in which you live thinks you're crazy. And the media which fill your ears and eyes tell you constantly that you owe it to yourself to be doing yourself more and more favors, and that, as you only go around once in life, you should be hitting it with all the gusto you can muster. On top of all that, you have a sinful and selfish heart which responds instinctively to all the self-interest philosophies being propagated so winsomely and compellingly around you. No wonder it takes deep-rooted strength to stand true to your heavenly calling in such an environment. But how good it is to remember that the Lord Jesus has been tempted in *all* points, and knows exactly what is involved in living a godly life. That is why He calls those who do it "great."

It would be a mistake to assume that the first disciples were only interested in being great. They were discussing who was going to be "the grea*test!*" It is conceivable that the disciples could have banded together to help each other improve their status in life. There would have been at least some degree of cooperation and teamwork involved if that had been the case. But they were into competition, not cooperation. They saw each other as stepping-stones, not building blocks. Few things are more destructive to developing relationships and building corporate effort than team strife and interpersonal tension.

But in a society where "winning is everything," where the survival of the fittest is an accepted tenet of life, and where the bottom line of the quarterly report often proves to be more significant than flesh and blood, disciples of Jesus Christ need to be constantly on their guard, lest they be caught in the "greatest" mindset and not realize that to go that route requires them to sacrifice some of the most gracious attributes of their Master.

Having spent a number of years in the business community before going into the ministry, I have no illusions about the difficulties that genuine disciples of Jesus Christ experience as they seek to live by His principles in an environment which is only too ready to take advantage of anything or anyone provided it will turn a profit, gain a toehold, or assure a move ahead. But from my own experience and that of many godly business people, I have observed the following:

1. I should set goals pleasing to the Master in the course of my daily business life. This will mean that work becomes worship and, accordingly, will be of the highest caliber. Work of the highest caliber is in and of itself of great worth and pays dividends.

2. Instead of seeking to beat the competition, I should compete against those attitudes and actions in my life which are displeasing to the Master and out of line with His dictates. This will greatly reduce undue stress and leave more energy for more important things.

3. I should strive to do only what the Master says and leave the results to Him. Since God has promised to care for those who walk uprightly, I can rest in the assurance that He will work in my circumstances and on my behalf.

These observations are not new, but they need to be reiterated constantly. It was my mother who taught me as I was about to embark on my business career, "Remember, Stuart, that God says, 'Those who honor Me, I will honor.'" I had no shortage of opportunities to put this principle to the test; and I know many others who have likewise chosen not to be the greatest on this earth, but will settle gladly for greatness in the kingdom. Indeed, many disciples of Jesus Christ are skillfully disguised as union men and business executives and homemakers. Whether in grimy factories, lofty office towers, or suburban split-levels, they are loyal and true to the Lord whatever their position. And it doesn't bother them at all if fame and riches pass them by, for the Master Himself thinks they are great!   ◆

Teach Us to Pray

PRAYER IS A UNIVERSAL PHENOMENON. I have watched hundreds of devout Jews—heads covered, clad in prayers shawls, rocking on the balls of their feet—as they prayed loudly and fervently at the western wall of the temple in Jerusalem. Not many yards away I have observed Muslims carefully going through ritualistic washings before prostrating themselves on their mats facing Mecca.

I have visited Buddhist shrines where crowds of worshipers bring fruit and burn joss sticks as robed priests lead them in prayer. I have listened to noisy crowds in Shinto shrines as they ring bells and light firecrackers to alert the spirits to their prayers. In great somber cathedrals, I have watched humble, gray-haired women light candles with work-ravaged hands before genuflecting and silently mouthing prayers of hope and desire.

I have knelt in prayer beside the dying, raised my arms in prayer with the ecstatics, joined my colleagues to pray for the healing of the sick, led vast stadium congregations in prayer, and quietly prayed with my wife for our children and their children. I have heard Presidents conclude their speeches with references to prayer and I have even heard TV anchormen remind us to keep hostages and famine victims "in our thoughts and prayers."

But while prayer is universally practiced, it is not universally understood. I remember having a long, interesting discussion with a professed atheist. As we were parting, I said to him, "I'm going to pray for you."

"Don't do that," he remonstrated hastily.

"Why not? As far as you're concerned, He's not there; so it can't do any harm."

"I know that. But I still don't want you praying for me."

"But tell me. Why not?" I insisted.

"Because I have a funny feeling it might work!"

Perhaps we are surprised to discover that atheists sometimes have "funny feelings" about prayer, but none of us is surprised to hear that people in tight corners believe in prayer. A man in a foxhole under fire once prayed, "God get me out of this and I'll never bother you again." God did and he didn't!

But is prayer a matter of ritual or superstition? Is it pious platitude or last resort? Do we engage in it as a matter of course, or is it an optional extra like whitewall tires, which make the automobile look good but don't materially affect its performance? These are questions which need to be examined by would-be disciples, because to a certain extent they also puzzled the original disciples.

Jesus prayed often, and His disciples knew it. He had sent them ahead in the boat while He prayed; and on more than one occasion He took some of them with Him to pray, though they didn't do very well. He had also made it quite clear to them that they were not to pray in the extravagant, unseemly manner of the hypocrites whose prayers were performances designed to impress men rather than petitions intended to implore God. He would have nothing to do with this kind of behavior.

One day a disciple came upon the Master praying in solitude. He waited till Jesus had finished and then said to Him, "Lord, teach us to pray, just as John taught his disciples" (Luke 11:1). The others gathered around and He instructed them to pray these words:

Father,
hallowed be Your name,

Your kingdom come.
Give us each day our daily bread.
Forgive us our sins,
for we also forgive everyone who sins against us.
And lead us not into temptation (vv. 2-4).

The Master had already taught the disciples this prayer during the Sermon on the Mount (see Matt. 6:9-13), but there are some differences between that account and the one here in Luke's gospel. This "repetition" serves to remind us of two things. One, the Lord's Prayer should not be regarded as just an illustration of the principles of prayer; it is a prayer to be prayed. Second, the different versions warn against a slavish repetition of words without due consideration for the intent of the content.

However, the disciples were clearly not satisfied that they were praying adequately and their request to be taught further was most appropriate. After all, disciples are learners and real learners never stop learning any more than real disciples stop developing. The request showed a genuine desire to experience more of the tranquility of spirit and sureness of purpose which they saw in the Master and which they rightly attributed to His communion with the Father through prayer.

The first lesson Christ taught His disciples was that prayer should be addressed to the Father. This may seem so obvious as to hardly merit mentioning, but it is sometimes overlooked that the effectiveness of prayer is not primarily related to the fervency of the one praying, but rather to the ability of the One prayed to, to hear and answer. Fervent prayer directed to the wrong object serves no useful purpose and in fact leads to all manner of ills. The Prophet Isaiah said, "Ignorant are those who carry about idols of wood, who pray to gods that cannot save" (Isa. 45:20).

Pity the one who prays fervently to a god who cannot save. And I'm not just thinking about those who live in remote regions of the world where the Gospel has not penetrated. I refer to the many who live in Christianized lands, whose knowledge of the Father is minimal and who therefore turn to Him seeking things He never offered, asking of Him things often contrary to His revealed will. Even committed disciples can fall into the trap of praying to One they have not taken the trouble to know; accordingly, they ask of Him things that He is not free to give.

Jesus used the Aramaic word *Abba* for "Father"—which interestingly enough is still the word a trusting young child in that part of the world would use in coming to his father. It speaks volumes about the character of the One to whom we come, and the attitude of the one coming to Him. Much about God as revealed in creation is awesome and perhaps intimidating: the One who rides on the wings of the storm and speaks with the voice of thunder is not to be ignored, but He is not to be avoided either. He has shown, primarily in Christ, that He is eminently approachable, deeply loving, and abounding in compassion toward those who genuinely seek Him and long to know Him. The Master reminded the disciples that even fallible earthly fathers know how to look after their children. If the kids ask for something appropriate, such as bread, Dad doesn't give them a useless stone; or if they ask for something nutritious, say a fish, he certainly doesn't give them a dangerous snake. That being the case, disciples should always recognize that their Heavenly Abba can be counted on to give them whatever is necessary for their greatest good—and they should live constantly with that assurance.

When our children were young, we lived in a very small house with inadequate facilities for study and quiet. So I had to find whatever quietish corner was available and do as much study as possible before the inevitable interruptions came from the kids. When they had something on their minds, they shared it! If they had a problem, they brought it! If they were excited about something, they shouted it! There was an openness about them that was delightful (except when I was pressured to finish something!), and there was a desire to share that was winsome and spontaneous. That is how children come to a father, and it is in that spirit that the disciples were encouraged to pray to their Abba.

First, Jesus taught the disciples that their prayers should be rightly directed; next, He taught that their prayers should be rightly formulated. If prayer is not mature, it will tend to be comprised mainly of requests—sometimes exclusively so! To understand prayer as a shopping list is to misunderstand prayer. Indeed, the one who prays "to get" is the one who misses much of what is to be experienced in prayer. True, children usually approach their fathers in terms of "Can I?" or "I want," or "Give me"—and this is perfectly understandable and legitimate—but it is also true that the most precious moments between father and child are more often couched in expressions like, "I love you, Daddy," or "Hold me, Daddy." In the same way, the Master taught His disciples to show, at the beginning of their prayers, that they were concerned *about Him* rather than about what they could get *from Him*. Notice the pronouns referring to God:

> Hallowed be *Your* name,
> *Your* kingdom come,
> *Your* will be done
> on earth as it is in heaven (Matt. 6:9-10).

There are two ways to have a conversation. One is to dive right in, tell the person all that you want him or her to know, and then leave. The other is to give the person the opportunity to tell you what he or she wants you to know while you listen carefully and then respond appropriately. The former is a conversation in name only and does very little to deepen a relationship, because one of the parties has shown little or no interest in the other. The latter is truly a conversation and serves to enrich the relationship between the participants, because each has been able to reveal what was in his or her heart and have someone else be interested enough to listen.

Prayer is the talking part of our relationship with God. When we come to the Lord expressing interest in His "name," "kingdom," and "will," we open ourselves up to the very real possibility of getting to know Him better, because we are identifying with the things on His heart.

Juliet wondered aloud to Romeo, "What's in a name?" But those who have learned the names of God know exactly what's in them. The varied aspects of the character of God are revealed in His names, and those who know that His character has been revealed want it to be truly represented and His reputation adequately protected. In other words, they want His name hallowed. To pray from the heart that you want God to be known as He truly is rather than as men have misunderstood and misrepresented Him—to long for people to recognize Him as the gracious One He has shown Himself to be—is to begin to pray aright.

To show concern about God's kingdom is to express dissatisfaction with the earthly status quo and a corresponding desire to see things put right by the only One capable of doing it. It speaks of a degree of estrangement from the present scene and a longing for that which is yet to come as the consummation of the divine plan. It betrays a kind of homesickness for eternity and glory, and a recognition that, while there is much that is wonderful about this present age, there is also much that grieves the heart of God and those who walk with His Son. To pray this way is to align the heart with the heart of God and to be quickened with His pulse beat.

To express a desire for God's will to be done on earth as it is in heaven presupposes some idea of how it is done in heaven and a willingness to be part of its implementation here on earth. The Master Himself had shown the disciples that He had come from heaven as a direct result of obedience to the Father's will; and He had so conducted Himself on earth that they had a clear idea of what doing the will of God meant, whether in heaven or on earth. There was a sense in which the prayer looked forward to a coming day when all the enemies of God would be vanquished, and His perfect will be done. But in the interim, they recognized that there should be an outworking of the will of God, as exemplified by the Master, in their own lives.

We noted earlier that it is perfectly normal for disciples to come to the Father like children, seeking from His hand what they need. But we have seen in the early parts of the Lord's Prayer that the heart of the disciple needs to be properly tuned to the heart of the Father if prayer is to be effective.

Assuming that we have practiced the discipline of coming
into His presence with a proper attitude, we then can be
confident that our requests are appropriate.

The Master specifically approved three types of requests:

> Give us today our daily bread.
> Forgive us our debts,
> as we also have forgiven our debtors.
> And lead us not into temptation,
> but deliver us from the evil one (Matt. 6:11-13).

♦ The first (daily bread) relates to physical needs.
♦ The second (forgiveness) has to do with relational needs.
♦ The third (temptation) refers to spiritual needs.

We humans have always had difficulty differentiating between "needs" and "wants"—and this causes prayer problems. God is committed to meeting "needs," but not necessarily "wants." "Daily bread," however, is about as basic as one
can get. How much butter and jam we may feel free to expect
from Him is left to the individual's conscience, but bread on
an ongoing basis is a legitimate need, and therefore a legitimate prayer item. This raises the matter of those who do not
even have enough basic necessities for survival, and strongly
suggests that such need should be not only a matter of prayer
but a cause for action.

"Forgiveness"—both in the sense of knowing what it is to
be forgiven and knowing what it means to forgive—is a most
significant subject for disciples. In God's way of thinking, the
word means simply to "no longer hold responsible," in the
same way that a person whose indebtedness is cancelled
(forgiven) is no longer required to deal with that indebtedness. The great need of the human race is to be freed from
responsibility for their sin against a Holy God. As He alone
can forgive sin, and then only on the basis of an adequate
satisfaction being made for sin, it follows that it is only
through His gracious initiative and action in Christ that man
can be released from sin's guilt and consequences. The good
news is that God is ready and eager to forgive those who
truly repent. It is right and proper, therefore, that disciple

should avail themselves of this forgiveness and live in the joyous good of it.

The other side of the coin requires that the forgiven be good forgivers. The Lord's Prayer does not suggest that forgiving others is the basis on which God forgives us. Rather, it reminds us that forgiveness is based on grace, but becomes operative in the lives of those who see their own unforgiving attitudes as sinful and turn from them. When forgiveness is adequately understood, relationships—both horizontal and vertical—are transformed. This should be a matter of continual desire and constant prayer.

That they were in a spiritual battle with evil forces was becoming increasingly apparent to the disciples of Jesus. So they were more and more aware that they were going to find themselves in situations which would give them every opportunity to go wrong. And that is what temptation is. But temptation is also an opportunity to do right, and that is why the Master allows us to be tempted or tested. The Lord's Prayer appears to be a request that the tempting and testing will be circumvented, if at all possible. The legitimacy of this kind of prayer is clear because the Master Himself prayed in a similar vein in the Garden of Gethsemane. He recognized, of course, that if the testing was unavoidable (and it wasn't), grace would be available (and it was). It is equally legitimate for disciples to pray that they will be delivered *from* temptation (i.e., not have to go through it); but if God knows that this is not in their best interests, then they should pray to be delivered *in* temptation (i.e., not be overcome by it). There has never been a disciple in any era who has not needed to pray constantly about this kind of thing.

I heard about a football coach who, after his team had won the championship, thought that they should offer thanks for the victory. So he told his players to kneel in the locker room, and, turning to one of his assistants, said, "You there. Pray the Lord's Prayer."

The assistant was as startled as his colleagues were amused. One of them nudged the man next to him and said, "Ten dollars says he doesn't know it!"

The assistant coach took off his hat, screwed it in his

hands, and started to pray, "Now I lay me down to sleep ..."

The coach who had made the bet was dumbfounded, fished in his pocket, and, as he handed over the money, said, "You could have fooled me. I didn't know he was religious!"

It is sad and amazing how many people revere the Lord's Prayer without knowing it. And it is tragic that some people who know it have failed to realize that this prayer, and all that it teaches, is crucial to the life of discipleship. ◆

On-the-Job Training

Since coming to live in America, I have often been asked, "Where did you get your education?" This question always sounds strange to me because it seems to suggest that my education (having been "got") must be complete. Thus I usually answer, "I'm still in the process of getting it."

"Oh, you're still going to school?"

"Yes."

"We didn't know that! Which school?"

"Life!"

"Oh, that's British humor, I suppose!"

Granted, there is a little British humor involved, but there also is a problem of international semantics. As we all know, the British and the Americans are two people divided by a common language. So when Americans talk about "education," they usually mean "school" or "college"; while the British try to differentiate between the two, perhaps because they suspect that many of those who come out of the British school system should not be confused with educated people!

In my case, my "schooling" finished at the age of seventeen, but my education is still underway. Because I started my professional career as a banker, it was necessary for me to start work in a bank immediately after I finished high school. For the next twelve years I never stopped learning, both in an academic sense—as I studied such exciting subjects as "Banking Law," "International Trade," and "Monetary Theory"—but also in a practical sense—as I learned how to handle people and errors, money and fraud, and many other things which have proved invaluable in the ministry! In my own experience, there has been much immensely valuable learning that is bookish, and much, equally valuable, that is people-, experience-, and life-oriented.

Discipleship is much the same. There is, no doubt, great benefit in programs designed to teach scriptural principles and spiritual values, but in the final analysis learning to be a disciple is a process more than a program. This becomes abundantly clear when we note the ways in which the Master, the Lord Jesus, took His disciples to school.

As Christ's impact increased, and as the religious leadership of the day had chance to find out exactly what He was doing, the tension built. The Pharisees were particularly incensed about Him, and eventually He took them on out in the open. The name *Pharisee*, which means literally "one who is separated," was applied to Jews who believed fervently in the levitical instructions concerning impurity. In their book, any contact with a "defiled" person transmitted "defilement" to them, and, as they believed just about everybody was "defiled," they had to live by the most stringent codes of behavior.

No doubt, like a lot of things, their approach had good beginnings. But human nature is such that their desire for purity had spawned corruption. The result was that the Pharisees, in their meticulous attention to external detail, had become unaware or unconcerned about their unpleasant internal attitudes—which were all too obvious to others, particularly to the Master. It was as if they were so busy polishing the apple that they were ignoring the worm. Jesus put it much more bluntly. He described them as "whitewashed tombs," and in case anyone missed the point, He added that they "look[ed] beautiful on the outside but on the inside are full of dead men's bones and everything unclean" (Matt. 23:27).

It is not surprising that the Pharisees did not take kindly to this kind of talk; indeed, their fury knew no bounds. Nor did it help that the Master's lifestyle was diametrically opposed to theirs. While they were meticulous about externals and gauged their righteousness by arbitrary measurements, the Master adopted a casual attitude to these standards. Instead, He majored on inner concerns of the heart: motives and attitudes, love and compassion. Jesus had no compunction about dining with "undesirables" such as tax collectors and prostitutes. What a marked contrast to the Pharisees whose attitude was, "We don't want them; they can only be detrimental to us."

The situation came to a head, and the Pharisees determined that Jesus was expendable. Their approach was to openly oppose Him as He taught, in the hope that they would be able to trap Him through skillful, devious questioning. If so, they could charge Him with blasphemy, and have Him done away with. Their problem was that Christ was always too quick on His feet for them, and this served only to increase their fury and determination.

While all this was going on, the crowds were gathering around to watch the fun, and, of course, to form opinions on both sides of the argument. Tempers were rising and the situation was getting very tense. Things got to such a pitch that on one occasion "a crowd of many thousands gathered" (Luke 12:1), to the point that people began to be literally trampled underfoot. Right in the middle of this mess stood the imperturbable Master and His perturbable disciples. In much the same way that a teaching surgeon coolly and calmly explains to his students exactly what he is doing, even when in the midst of a desperately serious procedure, so the Master took this opportunity to teach the disciples. It is what we call "on-the-job training."

Jesus got straight to the point with everybody listening. "Be on your guard against the yeast of the Pharisees, which is hypocrisy" (v. 17). *Hypocrisy* is such an unpleasant word. It literally means "to pretend" or "playact"—but with bad connotations.

One Sunday morning as I was driving home from church with my two younger children, I was unguarded enough to ask them, "What did you think about the sermon this morning?"

"It was fantastic, Dad," said Peter, going on to point out specific details which had impressed him.

"You hypocrite!" shouted my daughter with great emphasis.

"Judy, that's enough of that kind of talk. You will not call your brother a hypocrite," I reproved.

"OK, Dad, let me tell you what he did and then you tell me what kind of word to use!" she replied, unabashed. "He went into church with me, picked up a copy of the outline, sat on the back row, and memorized your three main points. Then he lay down and slept through the whole service. Just now you ask about the sermon—which he hadn't even heard—and he talks as if he knew all about it and enjoyed listening to it. Now you tell me what should I call him."

"Pete, is this true?" I asked, turning to look at my mildly embarrassed son.

"Yes, Dad. I was tired and your sermons are boring."

"There you are, Dad," said Judy. "Now what do we call him?"

"*Hypocrite*, unfortunately, is an appropriate word. But it is still a very unpleasant word to apply to anyone," I admitted reluctantly.

My daughter looked vindicated, my son slightly chastened, and I drove on trying to look firm and disapproving, but chuckling inside. In fact, feeling rather hypocritical myself!

The Master called hypocrisy "yeast," thereby graphically pointing out its insidious nature. As yeast works quietly and unobtrusively until it permeates everything, so hypocrisy's penchant for covering up reality and acting out a lie can become a way of life. This was certainly the case with the Pharisees. One example will suffice. The Pharisees quite rightly practiced tithing, but they took it to extremes. For instance, they would count out the stalks of garden herbs that they had grown, divide the number by ten, and give a tenth (a tithe) of the stalks to the Lord's work. The purpose of tithing, of course, was that it enabled the giver to show how much he recognized that all that he had was attributable to God's grace; thus the giving of the tithe was an expression of loving gratitude. In addition, the gift made nourishment available to others who were otherwise impoverished.

But Jesus pointed out that the ritualistic observance itself had become so all-consuming that the Pharisees had lost interest in loving the Lord and other people, and seeing that justice was done. Being loving and acting justly are both harder to do and more difficult to evaluate than sets of rules that must be obeyed. If the outward acts are a true expression of love for God and people, and a commitment to seeing that justice is done, they are of great worth. But if the outward acts purport to be what they are not, and, in addition, have become a substitute for inner reality, they are abominable. Disciples through the centuries have needed to be on their guard against such hypocrisy.

But why do we have this tendency to project what is false and to cover up what is really in our hearts? No doubt, this question has many answers, but Christ implied that one major reason is that we are often so concerned about what people think of us that we will go to great lengths to put on a performance for them—even to the extent of acting out what is palpably untrue. He went on to suggest that wrapped up in this concern is an element of fear; in the case of His original disciples, a fear of death at the hands of their enemies. Given the tense circumstances under which He told them these things, it would appear that their fears may have been well-founded! Perhaps He sensed that some of them under that kind of duress might play a role to save their skins. But He quickly put the picture into perspective for them, saying, "But I will show you whom you should fear: Fear Him who, after the killing of the body, has power to throw you into hell. Yes, I tell you, fear Him" (Luke 12:5).

The tragedy of all hypocrisy is that it illustrates the hypocrite is more concerned about what man thinks than about what God knows; is more worried about what man might do than what God could do; and is more interested in the immediate circumstances, where man resides, than the ultimate glory, in which God reigns.

There was (and still is) a danger of hypocrisy working in two entirely different ways. On the one hand, some people might believe in their hearts, but be afraid to confess they are following the Lord. To such men and women, Jesus said, "He who disowns Me before men will be disowned before the angels of God" (12:9). On the other hand, there may be those who, for whatever reason, might wish to be accepted as genuine believers, but whose hearts are actually far from the Lord. To them, He will one day say, "I don't know you or where you come from. Away from Me, all you evildoers" (13:27).

Peter would later be guilty of both kinds of hypocrisy. When, after the Lord's arrest, he was faced with the servant girl's challenge that he was a follower of the Master, Peter replied, "Woman, I don't know Him" (22:57). This after three years with the Master!

Years later he was in trouble again. After the Apostle Paul had preached successfully in Galatia, a controversy erupted as to whether the new converts needed to become adherents of Judaism and participate in all its rituals and ceremonies. Some said that if they didn't participate, they were not really numbered among the people of God; others (Paul and Peter included) insisted that not only was it *not* necessary for the new converts to adhere to Judaism, but for them to do so would be most detrimental to their understanding of Christ and the furtherance of the Christian mission. But when Peter was among some of his old Jewish friends who were in the other camp, he began to waver—despite the fact that he previously had taken a stand against their position. When Paul found out about this, he was furious and "opposed him to his face, because he was in the wrong" (Gal. 2:11).

In both instances, Peter capitulated to the fear of men despite being fully aware that the Lord knew his heart, would be deeply hurt by his hypocrisy, and deeply distressed that His cause would be jeopardized as a result. These were the very things about which the Master had warned His disciples, but, like their successors, they didn't always learn as quickly and thoroughly as they ought.

Given our natural tendency to play roles that do not always equate with reality, we should ask what safeguards to take against such behavior. The first, we have already seen, is to be aware of the propensity. Forewarned should always be forearmed!

Second, as we have also seen, is to be constantly aware that the Lord knows our hearts and is far more significant than any person we may wish to impress.

Third, we should recognize the great care our Heavenly Father extends toward us. Reminding the disciples that sparrows are practically worthless in terms of economics, yet never beyond the Father's care, Jesus points out His far greater concern and compassion for men and women, boys and girls (Luke 12:6). This knowledge should serve to warm the disciple's heart and accordingly protect it from hypocritical activities.

Fourth, those who tempt disciples to cover up the reality of their heart's devotion are those who fall into the category of "blaspheming against the Holy Spirit" (12:10), an unforgivable sin. By this, Jesus meant that those who willfully reject the overtures of the Holy Spirit in their lives to such an extent that they not only resist the truth, but violently deny its authenticity, attributing His gracious work to Satan instead, shall find no basis for forgiveness. It follows that those who deny the only means of reconciliation to God are left without means of forgiveness. The point for us disciples appears to be that we should not be so intimidated by such people that we become tempted to playact. Rather, we should have such a desire to rescue unbelievers before they finally settle into this pernicious attitude that we would openly and consistently declare our discipleship in word and deed.

The Master, knowing what lay ahead of Him, was equally aware of the trauma that awaited His followers. Jesus had already stated that He would stand before the authorities in Jerusalem, be found guilty, and pay with His life. But now He was intimating that a similar fate awaited them. No doubt it went over the disciples' heads, like many of the other things He told them; but perhaps a grain of truth lodged in their minds—truth which came to fruition when the events actually took place. He told them, "When you are brought before synagogues, rulers, and authorities, do not worry about how you will defend yourselves or what you will say, for the Holy Spirit will teach you at that time what you should say" (12:11-12).

Some time later, Peter and John found themselves in this exact situation and they acquitted themselves so well that the authorities looked quite foolish and inept. Luke recalls, "When they [the authorities] saw the courage of Peter and John and realized that they were unschooled, ordinary men, they were astonished and they took note that these men had been with Jesus" (Acts 4:13). This did not save Peter and John from some difficult experiences, but it did mean they had been saved from hypocrisy. And the result was great blessing for all concerned.

Centuries later, Martin Luther stood before a similar tribunal in the city of Worms. Challenged to recant his controversial beliefs and to withdraw his many statements and writings, he answered, "My conscience is captive to the Word of God. I will not recant anything, for to go against conscience is neither honest nor safe. Here I stand; I cannot do otherwise. God help me. Amen."

Of course, citing Peter and John before the Sanhedrin, and Luther before the Diet at Worms is to be far removed from the place where most modern disciples live. It is true that large numbers are in physical danger because of their faith, and thousands in recent days have laid down their lives rather than yield to hypocrisy. But the majority of disciples are never placed in such threatening situations, are never tempted to play a game for survival. Temptations, for us, are more subtle.

How many disciples of Christ have carefully avoided stating their convictions at a job interview for fear of losing a possible promotion? And how many young men and women have allowed their affections to so control them that they have never openly admitted their Christianity to the one to whom they are attracted?

Eric Liddell was a man who knew what was in his heart and allowed it to flow from his lips. The result was that when, as a member of the 1924 British Olympic team, he discovered that his race was to be run on a Sunday, he declined to compete. Intense pressure was brought to bear upon him. He was the talk of the Paris games. Even the Prince of Wales and the British Olympic Committee tried to dissuade him. To no avail. He stood firm, despite the fact that, as world record holder, he was favored to win the gold medal. Liddell did run another race later in the games and won, but he didn't run against his convictions. No hypocrite, he. When he died at the age of forty-three in a Japanese prison camp during World War II, a leading Scottish newspaper wrote, "Scotland has lost a son who did her proud every hour of his life." Here, truly, was a disciple of Jesus Christ skillfully disguised as an Olympic gold medalist, missionary, and patriot.   ♦

Possessions

I ONCE SPOKE AT A SPECIAL series of meetings in a church in
North Carolina. The host pastor was particularly anxious that
I should answer questions on the final evening and made
announcements each night to remind people to come with
their questions. The great day arrived, the question-and-
answer time was announced, and I awaited the first question.
And I waited. And I waited. Finally, a little lady put up her
hand rather tentatively and said, "I've got a question for ya."

"Good. Go ahead," I said, somewhat relieved.

"I've listened to ya every night this week and there's something botherin' me."

"Well, let's see if we can deal with your problem," I
answered.

She hesitated for a moment, then asked, "Is them yer own
teeth?"

I assured her that they were my own, because my mother
gave them to me! But it took a while before we could restore
some semblance of order to the proceedings. I thought afterward that if that episode hadn't been so funny, it would have
been very frustrating! I'd spent a whole week teaching the
people, trying to lead them on in their walk with the Lord,
and she had not gotten past my teeth! But then I remembered
that it has always been like this. Even the Master Himself
experienced similar problems.

After Jesus had dealt with such subjects as hypocrisy, being cast into hell, and the unforgivable sin of blasphemy against the Holy Spirit, somebody in the crowd shouted out, "Teacher, tell my brother to divide the inheritance with me" (Luke 12:13). This showed where his interests lay, and they certainly weren't even close to the significant matters that the Master had been addressing. But Christ did not miss the opportunity to use the situation as yet another teaching experience. No doubt the disciples were aware of this, and in later years, developed skills in taking the situations presented to them and turning them into occasions to communicate the truth.

Jesus refused to get into the debate apparently raging between the two brothers concerning the division of property which had been left to them. Evidently, even in those days the principle applied, "Where there's a will, there's a quarrel!" The man who felt he was being shortchanged saw a public exposure of his brother as a great chance to press his case and perhaps embarrass his sibling into an action which would achieve his own selfish ends. But the Master quickly saw the root problem and did not hesitate to address it, not only for the benefit of the brothers, but also for the benefit of His disciples and the crowds still gathered around Him. "Watch out!" He said. "Be on your guard against all kinds of greed; a man's life does not consist in the abundance of his possessions" (12:15). The problem with the brother who wanted his money was apparently the same as with the brother who didn't want him to have it! Greed! It was ever thus.

Two kinds of people live in this world—the "haves" and the "have nots." The "haves" have what the "have nots" have not. The "have nots" want what the "haves" have, but the "haves" have no intention of letting the "have nots" have what they "have not." It's simpler to understand than to say!

The difficulty is that mankind, being part material and part spiritual, is required to live spiritually in a material world. In ancient days, there were those who believed that material things were intrinsically evil, and should therefore be shunned. The extent to which one was able to deprive oneself of possessions determined the degree of spirituality achieved.

But this approach has one fatal flaw—material cannot possibly be evil. First, because God created it, and when He had concluded His Creation, He declared it very good. Second, because God in Christ assumed our humanity, being born of a virgin and becoming flesh. So, in fact, to suggest such a philosophy, even in the name of deep spirituality, is to deny that God could have become incarnate for our redemption and also to deny that He has given us all things richly to enjoy.

On the other hand, especially in the modern era, we have to contend with the attitude that material is everything. The spirit of the age is expressed starkly in the saying, "The best things in life are things." And it is no surprise that this principle is pushed to the conclusion that even more things are even better. And more and more things are even better, and so on, *ad infinitum.* Even if people do not subscribe to this philosophy, it is difficult for them not to be affected by it because of the environment in which they live.

Our society is committed to the idea that economies should grow so that more and more people can enjoy a better standard of living. This seems appropriate, but there is a hidden hook to the idea which needs to be recognized. Economies grow as production increases. Production increases as demand expands. Demand expands as it is stimulated. Stimulation is achieved by addressing inbred psychological factors to the point of manipulation and exploitation. So advertising, which can be an immensely helpful tool, has instead become a powerful weapon playing on such human factors as fear, pride, desire, and greed. And if people cannot afford these "necessities of life," credit is always available; they can have the goods now and pay later. Thus we find the natural human desires to acquire goods, to be accepted, and to have positive feelings about oneself perverted and turned against us. Material, far from being regarded as evil, is close to being reckoned as everything.

In case we might be tempted to think that this is a totally new development, it is good to remember that over a hundred years ago Alexis de Tocqueville wrote in his famous book *Democracy in America,* "No stigma attaches to the love of money in America, and provided it does not exceed the bounds imposed by public order, it is held in honor. The American will describe as noble and estimable what our medieval ancestors would have called base cupidity."

Ivan Boesky said, "Greed is healthy." Jesus taught, "Be on your guard against all kinds of greed." De Tocqueville wrote, "No stigma attaches to the love of money in America." The Apostle Paul warned, "The love of money is a root of all kinds of evil" (1 Tim. 6:10). Yes, there is a clear tension between the commonly accepted view of our society and the teaching of Scripture at this point, and this requires that modern-day disciples think clearly about what they truly believe on the subject of materialism.

Between the poles where material is regarded as either evil or everything—both of which positions are repudiated by Scripture—a balance must exist. And Jesus told a parable about a successful farmer, designed to demonstrate that balance. This farmer, when considering his abundant resources, decided he had done so well that he would conserve his assets and live off them to the fullest. His idea of the good life was, "Take life easy; eat, drink, and be merry" (Luke 12:19). However, he had become so engrossed with material things that he had overlooked the major issues of life. So God called him a fool, told him that he would die rather than enjoy the fruits of his labor, and asked, "Then who will get what you have prepared for yourself?" (v. 20) Turning to the assembled crowd, the Master added the punch line, "This is how it will be with anyone who stores up things for himself but is not rich toward God" (v. 21).

At no time did the Master criticize the farmer for being successful or for having considerable resources. The criticism was that he had stored everything up for himself and was not rich toward God. We need, therefore, to recognize that material things *can* rightfully be owned, used, and enjoyed, but they *cannot* be stored up without reference to their appropriate place in our lives. Perhaps even more importantly, we must recognize that material things can become so demanding and compelling that they deviate our attention from the things that are much more significant. Thus the key questions become: "How do we guard against material things becoming

dominant in our lives?" and, "What *is* the proper place of
material things, which are part of the life God has given us to
live as disciples?"

We guard against a materialistic outlook by concentrating
on being rich toward God. This means we place priority on
things that really matter. Paul told us that when everything
else had passed away, three things would remain: namely,
"faith, hope and love. But the greatest of these is love"
(1 Cor. 13:13). Love stands the test of time and outlasts material things which moths, rust, and thieves tend to destroy. But
the tragedy for many moderns is that they are so busy with
the things that they have little or no time for the loving. How
many marriages have collapsed for no other reason than the
couple became so engrossed in amassing what they believed
they needed for the good life that they found nothing was left
that was good in their life? How many busy, successful people have been anything but successful in their attempts to
bring up a family because they provided things *for* their children, but never gave themselves lovingly *to* their children?

But if love for people is lasting, what can we say of love for
God? How sad it is to see the man who is so busy making a
pile which he will soon leave that he has no time at all for the
God whom he will shortly meet! What a tragedy it is to watch
the man who, given every opportunity to love God, loves
things more; and finishes crushed under the load of his own
acquisitions, as his life drains out in bitterness and loneliness!

In his first epistle, Peter wrote about another lasting quality
which, although he specifically applied it to women, does not
exclusively belong to the female sex. He wrote about "the
unfading beauty of a gentle and quiet spirit, which is of great
worth in God's sight" (1 Peter 3:4). Something which is of
great worth in God's sight needs to be valued highly by hu-
mankind. Unfortunately, as we have seen all too often in our
day and age, the scramble for material things has not only
superseded the desire for quality character, but in many instances has made the development of quality character practically impossible. How many initially gracious people have
become tough and cynical because they found that to acquire
"necessities" they must aggressively pursue a course of

action which they themselves disapprove of? No wonder Paul warned about the love of money, and the Master cautioned against greed!

But what are the safeguards? The Lord went on to explain that the best way to ensure that material things do not become your god is to use your resources in the service of God. He used dramatic instructions such as, "Sell your possessions and give to the poor," adding that the result would be "purses that would not wear out, a treasure in heaven" (Luke 12:33). The extent to which this is done must be determined by the individual disciple, but the principle is clear. We know that the Master said, "It is more blessed to give than to receive" (Acts 20:35). But it takes a certain degree of spiritual maturity to believe it, and that is why it has often been said that the last thing to be converted is the pocketbook.

Some years ago, Jill and I conducted a series of meetings in Belfast, Northern Ireland. On the last day of our stay, which happened to be my birthday, we went out for dinner after the service with Bill and Eleanor Fitch, dear friends of long standing. During the course of the meal, the police telephoned Bill to tell him that terrorists had entered his office block, held his night watchman at gunpoint, and filled the building with explosive and incendiary devices. Bill thanked him for the information, returned to the table, told us what had happened; and then, when we suggested we should leave right away, said calmly, "No, let's have dessert and coffee first!"

When we finally arrived, we found a scene of devastation, and spent most of the rest of the night raking through the smoking wreckage looking for things which might be salvageable. During this whole time, I watched Bill going about his work quietly and uncomplainingly. Long into the night, when many other office owners in the same block had arrived on the scene, he called everybody together. Some had apparently been at a wild party and were the worse for drink; some had obviously been wakened from their sleep; others were standing there quietly weeping as if stunned by what had happened. My friend said to them, "Friends, this is a sad moment for us all. But it is now the early hours of the Lord's Day. So I suggest we all go home to our beds, get some sleep, and wake refreshed so that we might be found in the house of the Lord on His day. Although we have lost much, we have so much for which to thank Him, and tomorrow we should make a fresh start in acknowledging Him for all His goodness. So let us pray together, and then off you go to your beds."

To my surprise, Bill's fellow businessmen listened carefully to what he had to say, and when he was through, they thanked him, quietly filed out, and went home. I have no idea how many were in a place of worship the next day, but I do know one thing. I had stood that night in a burned-out building with a man who knew how to lay up treasure in heaven, even though he operates constantly in the heady realms of high finance where many a man has fouled up his life by greed. He was that night a disciple of Jesus Christ skillfully disguised under layers of soot and grime as a high financier.

♦

How to Recognize a Disciple

THE MASTER ISSUED no uniforms to His disciples. He gave them no ID badges. But this was not because He wanted them to be incognito. On the contrary, He wanted them to be readily recognizable. In fact, He stipulated two specific ways of ensuring this very thing. Note two verses from John's gospel: "All men will know that you are My disciples if you love one another" (13:35); "This is to My Father's glory, that you bear much fruit, showing yourselves to be My disciples" (15:8). Both of these highly significant expressions require considerable thought because, while they are easy to articulate, they are not at all easy to understand or implement.

Fortunately, Jesus amplified what He meant in striking fashion. Talking about love as the hallmark of a disciple, He gave the Twelve a fitting analogy: "As I have loved you, so you must love one another" (John 13:34). That statement alone immediately got the idea of loving out of the amorphous abstract into the down-to-earth practical, because every one of those disciples could point to specific ways that Christ's love for them had taken on form and content.

All of the disciples had just witnessed something that was extraordinary, even by the dramatic standards to which they were, by this time, becoming accustomed. They had gone out together for the Passover meal. Normal custom required that a slave or woman (in those days they had problems differen-

tiating between the two!) kneel before the guests to wash the
dust and mire of the journey from their feet. But on this
particular occasion, no slave or woman showed up to do the
honors. Perhaps the slave had joined a union and the woman
had gone to hear Gloria Steinem! Whatever the reason, proto-
col required that the most junior member of the group pick
up the slack and do the job.

Apparently no one wanted to admit to being the junior, so
the feet were left unwashed. This was unacceptable to the
Master for reasons both obvious and not. Obviously, the at-
mosphere would be greatly enhanced by the liberal application of soap and water; but more importantly, the disciples'
attitudes needed cleaning up too. So the Master assumed the
servant role and proceeded to do what no one else was prepared to do. He started to wash feet. He was not trying to
shame or embarrass the disciples, though He no doubt did it
anyway. As John records, by washing their feet, "He now
showed them the full extent of His love" (13:1). The point is
that they were to love others as He loved them—and He was
showing them that loving means serving.

When Jesus arrived at Peter's feet, He ran into a problem,
of course. Peter refused to allow the Master to do such menial service, only to be told, "You do not realize now what I
am doing, but later you will understand" (v. 7). This may, at
first sight, appear to elevate a delightfully humble action a
little too highly. But as the conversation develops, it becomes
apparent that the Master was saying, in effect, "Peter, I am
washing dirty feet with water right now, but shortly I will be
washing away sin with My blood." It was both the water and
the blood as cleansing agents which the Lord would adminis-
ter in humble servanthood. The full extent of His love was
shown in rough outline washing feet, but in full color washing
away sin. It is obvious that we could never be called upon to
offer a sacrifice that would expiate sins, either our own or
those of anyone else. But it is equally obvious that humble
service in the name of Christ is a required mark of discipleship. It is interesting to note that while the modern media do
not hesitate to hold up to ridicule the foibles of errant ministers, they universally speak with great respect of Mother

Teresa, the Slavic nun who has devoted her life to ministering to the underprivileged and desperately needy. I suspect that few people, even among the most cynical, would dispute her claim to be a disciple, but I fear that there are many who would laugh out of court similar claims from others who show more love for publicity and power than for people.

Talk is cheap; love is hard work, particularly when it involves doing humble, menial, servant tasks. It is not uncommon for believers to make loud claims to love, but at the same time to be reluctant to serve. When this happens, spiritual corrective surgery is in order.

My dad used to tell the story of a man who, at his wife's urging, bought an electric bell and installed it on his front door. When the installation was completed, he connected the wires to a battery, called his wife to his side, pressed the button—and the bell rang out loud and clear. His wife, sensing the time was ripe, then said, "All we need now is a light over the front door so people can see the doorbell." With a typical masculine sigh, the man returned to the store, bought the light, fixed the wiring, attached it to the battery, and with a flourish flicked the switch. But nothing happened. Crestfallen, he checked everything and tried again, with the same negative results. Having depleted the resources of his electrical knowledge, he called a friend and explained what had happened. His friend was amazed that he had linked both the bell and the light to a battery, pointing out that the battery might be powerful enough to ring a bell, but not to shine a light. Said he, "You see, it takes a lot more power to shine than to shout!"

Elizabeth Barrett Browning asked the question, "How do I love thee? Let me count the ways." Then she proceeded to enumerate in classical poetic language the "depth and breadth and height" of her love. Less poetic souls need look only at the ways they are eager to serve, as opposed to the ways in which they expect to be served, in order to evaluate how well they demonstrate love.

One of the twelve disciples, never identified for us, was known specifically as "the disciple whom Jesus loved" (John 21:20). The context reveals that he was not Peter, so it is generally accepted, for reasons we do not need to explore at this point, that he was John. This has led many people to assume that John must have been a particularly sweet character who drew out of the Master a special love unlike the love He had for the rest of the group. But the facts do not bear this out.

There is no doubt that John was particularly loving in his old age. His epistles are dominated by the love theme, and tradition tells us that when he was approaching 100 years of age, he would be carried into the assembly of believers in Ephesus and say to them, "Brethren, love one another." Indeed, because he rarely gave the Ephesian Christians any other advice, someone asked John why he had nothing else to tell them, a question to which he reputedly replied, "Because there is nothing else to say!" But while such was true of John the old man, it was not true of John in his youth.

Remember that the Lord once gave John and his brother James the nickname, "Sons of Thunder." This presumably referred to the tempestuous way in which they reacted to situations and the stormy relationships which they experienced. As we have already seen, John was quick to demand fire and brimstone be rained on the Samaritan villages that did not welcome the disciples, and he was not at all reluctant to rebuke a healer who was not among the Master's immediate followers. But perhaps the most telling thing about John's youthful character was that he, his brother, and mother made overtures to Christ concerning the highest places of honor in the kingdom, which they assumed He was about to establish. The picture that emerges from all the evidence is not one of a loving, caring, humble servant, but of an arrogant, bad-tempered, intolerant, tunnel-visioned upstart! This was the disciple whom Jesus loved!

It takes the eye and imagination of a sculptor to look at a block of masonry and "see" in it a work of art. But it also takes much patient chipping away over long tedious hours before the work is completed. In the same way, the Master apparently saw things in the youthful John which were hidden to everyone else (with the possible exception of his mother!). But it took years of patient working with him before the unattractive aspects fell away and the transformed disciple began to appear. This work was begun in John as the two of them walked the roads together, but it was continued by the Spirit who worked a patient miracle from within. Loving as Christ loved His disciples includes having vision enough to see potential in people and patience enough to see the potential realized.

A number of women in our congregation are married to men who have been less than ideal husbands, and that's putting it mildly. Some of these men are alcoholics who squander money on booze while denying it to necessities. Their wives have taken on extra work to make up for the shortfall in resources and keep the family warm and fed. They have often nursed their men when they are ill. The capacity for love and patience in these women has been a source of wonderment to me, and it has been a reflection of their discipleship. I realize, of course, that women such as these are sometimes called "facilitators," and that they are often detrimental to their own desire to see transformation in their spouses' lives. But having said that, there still is something wonderful about loving that patiently works with the unpromising and the unresponsive until, in the end, victory is won. This was how the Master loved John, and He told us to use His love as our model.

In Bethany there was a small home which proved to be a haven for the Lord. We don't know how often He went there, but we do know that Lazarus, Mary, and Martha—whose home it was—were very special to Him, and He was always welcome there. In fact, we are told specifically that "Jesus loved Martha and her sister and Lazarus" (John 11:5). But all was not well in the family. On one of the Master's visits, Martha was busy getting supper ready, while the Master and Mary apparently were having a Bible study together. Martha began to get very irritated about this state of affairs and eventually said to the Master, "Lord, don't You care that my sister has left me to do the work by myself? Tell her to help me!" (Luke 10:40)

At this point it is interesting to see how He expressed His love for both these women. Very gently but firmly He pointed out to Martha, "You are worried and upset about many things, but only one thing is needed" (v. 41). No doubt she knew she was upset without Him telling her, but she at least sensed that He understood her and probably asked Him, "What then is the one thing that is needed?" Some scholars have suggested the Master meant that the elaborate meal Martha was preparing was really not necessary, and that one course would be sufficient. Others suggest—and I agree—that His statement was pointing to a need for a more spiritual approach on her part. Whatever He meant, we do know that Martha was confronted but consoled—lovingly.

Meanwhile Mary was probably happily listening to all that transpired and perhaps even taking notes on how the Master was handling the situation! Note that Jesus endorsed her interest in learning at His feet and said, "Mary has chosen what is better, and it will not be taken away from her" (v. 41). Recall too that the rabbis were totally opposed to teaching the Torah to women, saying among other things, "Every man who teaches his daughter Torah is as if he taught her promiscuity," and, "Let the words of Torah be burned up, but let them not be delivered to women."

Perhaps the problem between the two women was not just one of temperament, although that certainly appears to have been part of it. It looks to me as if Mary was responding to the Master's new, untraditional approach to women; He was bringing them out of the shadows and establishing for them the place in society that Creation had ordained for them, but which the consequences of the Fall had denied them. But women like Martha, who was probably more of a traditionalist, were resistant to such a notion and still believed that "a woman's place is in the kitchen." We should have no difficulty understanding this, because the same tensions exist to this day. Nonetheless, Jesus loved these sisters, empathized with their desires and frustrations, and endeavored to meet each at the point of her own uniqueness.

A major lesson is found here for modern disciples. The loving thing to do in a tense situation is to try to discover why people are doing what they are doing, instead of reacting to what they are doing! It is relatively easy, and usually disastrous, to respond to what people say or do without taking the trouble to ask, and if possible answer, the question, "Why on earth would they do that?" Love tries hard to understand.

One more illustration of the Master's love and what it teaches about the way disciples love will suffice. A wealthy young man rushed up to Christ one day and, throwing himself at His feet, said, "Good teacher, what must I do to inherit eternal life?" (Mark 10:17) First, Jesus reminded him to keep the commandments, which the man avowed that he had done since he was a boy. So then Jesus told him to sell everything he owned, give the proceeds to the poor, and follow Him. This was too much for the young man, who obviously had not kept the commandment to love God with all his heart and his neighbor as himself. As he sadly walked away, the Lord "looked at him and loved him" (v. 21). The Master's love for this man welled out despite the fact that he was in the process of walking away. Jesus did not plead with him, run after him, or alter the terms of blessing so as not to lose him. To have done any of these things would have trivialized the significance of eternal life as well as the dignity, responsibility, and accountability of mankind.

When the disciples love those who do not follow their Master, they show it by having the deepest concern for their spiritual well-being. They deal with the issues fairly and squarely, and they treat unbelievers with the greatest courtesy and respect. Sometimes I have wondered if, in our excessive desire to "win people to Christ," some of us have failed in this regard. Unbelievers quite often raise what they genuinely regard as valid objections to the Gospel. When this occurs, the loving thing to do is to listen intently and try hard to understand where they are coming from, not to interrupt them with a stock biblical answer—which may be compelling to a disciple of long standing, but of no relevance whatsoever to someone with little or no knowledge of the things of God.

In the same way, getting people to respond to a minimal presentation of the message of Christ without giving them the chance to assimilate the truth and think through the consequences may show more concern for the scalp of another convert than genuine love for the person as a person.

The Master held Himself before the disciples as an example to emulate: "As I have loved you, so you must love one another." But the challenge is so great and the consequences so far reaching that there is always a tendency for us to treat such a statement with benign neglect, as if to say tacitly, "It is truly a wonderful concept and the world would be a better place if it worked. But there's the rub. It won't work. It's just too much!" I offer two responses to this reaction.

First, Jesus did not ask us to consider a possible approach to see if we thought it was practical. He said, "A new *commandment* I give you: Love one another" (John 13:34, italics added). Commandment is not suggestion!

Second, this teaching was given about the time Jesus introduced the disciples to the ministry of the Holy Spirit. Among other things, they were going to learn that loving as the Master loved required obedience to His command when they didn't feel like being obedient; plus it meant dependence upon the Holy Spirit to work in them continually, because they would always find themselves inadequate. It is only through obedience and dependence that the capacity to love as commanded becomes even a remote possibility.

There is a remarkable woman in our congregation named Win Couchman. I think I could write a book about her, but a few sentences will suffice to say that she has been to me a constant example of what it really means to love people. She is patient with them, always tries to understand them, sees their potential, relates to where they are coming from, senses what they are feeling, is always available, and never does anything to abuse their dignity. But she is firm when necessary, and tough if need be. She can minister to ministers and care for castaways. The up-and-outers look up to her and the down-and-outers find her on their level. A few years ago, she and her husband Bob, who displays many similar characteristics, took an early retirement and embarked on an exciting new career working as counselors and friends with young short-term missionaries. Win and Bob have literally roamed the world loving and caring. You could certainly call them disciples of Jesus Christ skillfully disguised as early retirees.

♦

You'll Know Them by Their Fruit

A FRIEND OF MINE USED to tell this story about his childhood. He and his brothers, like most boys, were occasionally reprimanded by their parents and sent to their rooms as punishment. In their case, the punishment didn't really work because they had devised a method to escape detention—an old fruit tree that stood outside their bedroom window. Once banished to their room, they would quietly open the window, climb down the tree, and play in the fields behind their home before returning. One day they heard their father tell their mother that because the fruit tree was no longer bearing any fruit, he proposed chopping it down. Realizing that this could seriously jeopardize their lifestyles, the young boys decided immediate action should be taken; so pooling their pocket money, they dashed to the village, bought apples and black thread, and late that evening busily tied apples all over the tree. (My friend assured me the story was true!) Next morning they waited with baited breath for their parents' response, and soon they heard their father call to their mother, "Mary, the most remarkable thing has happened! The fruit tree that bore no fruit for years is covered with apples this morning. I don't believe it. It's a miracle!"

The boys beamed with pleasure, knowing that the tree and their escape route were saved. But their smiles faded when they heard Dad add, "I don't believe it, because it's a pear tree!"

Like many wise parents, my friend's parents had apparently been turning a blind eye to their sons' capers for some time! They also showed their wisdom and rare good humor by allowing the tree to survive. The point of the story, however, is as simple as it is obvious. Pears don't grow on apple trees and vice versa. That being true, if you do see apples growing on a tree, it is reasonable to assume that you are looking at an apple tree.

The Lord Jesus made a similar inescapable point when in effect He told the disciples that the best way to identify a disciple is to take a good look at what is growing on the outside. His exact words were, "This is to My Father's glory, that you bear much fruit, showing yourselves to be My disciples" (John 15:8). It follows, therefore, that all disciples should have a working knowledge of the nature of this fruit and how it is cultivated.

Interestingly enough, the Master made no attempt, in this context, to define what He meant by *fruit*, so we must believe that He intended the most obvious interpretation. We might ask ourselves the question, "What exactly is fruit?" The answer I suggest is, "Fruit is the outward evidence of inner life." Tying apples on pear trees doesn't work because real fruit is not artificially attached. Fruit is a natural outgrowth; the growth is related to the life. That is why "pear" life doesn't produce "apple" fruit.

What then is the life that uniquely indwells the disciple and which demonstrates itself through him? Christ explained that quite clearly: "I am the vine, you are the branches. If a man remains in Me and I in him, he will bear much fruit; apart from Me you can do nothing" (15:5). Put in the simplest terms, disciples prove they are disciples by the way their lives show something of the characteristics of Christ Himself, as His life shines through theirs.

As Jesus introduced this section of teaching, He said, "I am the true vine" (15:1), with particular emphasis on the word *true*. The disciples were certain to recognize the significance of this emphasis, even though it may not be as obvious to us. Israel was often referred to as "the vine" in the Old Testament, usually in terms of its failure to be productive. For instance, Jehovah told His ancient people through the Prophet Jeremiah: "I had planted you like a choice vine of sound and reliable stock. How then did you turn against Me into a corrupt, wild vine?" (Jer. 2:21) In other words, as the prophets had done before Him, the Master was not only deploring the abject failure of Israel to be what God intended, but He was also stating that He Himself would produce what Israel had never produced. What Israel with her nationalism, her religious structures, and her Law had not produced He promised to reproduce in His disciples. This was a claim so radical as to be either utter blasphemy or profound truth.

Try, if you can, to put yourself in the disciples' sandals as they, proud adherents of Judaism, heard Him make these startling assertions. Perhaps it might be easier for us to grasp what He was saying if we remember that John Wesley—with his proud Christian heritage, his disciplined and devout lifestyle at Oxford, his compassionate and methodical care for the underprivileged, and his courageous commitment to reaching the American Indians—still found himself to be spiritually barren until he discovered, through his Aldersgate experience, that his focus must be on Christ Himself.

Let's bring it closer to home. Try to imagine what it means to a proud Britisher to be told that being born in a nation that for centuries has traditionally stood for what's right; being an adherent of a classy, sophisticated, and erudite Anglicanism; and having the impeccable manners, breeding, and refinements of the classic English gentleman will never of themselves produce discipleship! Or try telling a beautiful, young woman full of Southern charm and grace—whose father built the local Presbyterian church, who devotes her considerable organizational abilities and country-club contacts to opposing "atheistic communism," "the liberal establishment in Washington," pornography, and abortion—that it takes Christ to be a disciple. This was the emphasis the Master was bringing then and still brings today. And as if to reinforce His statement, the Lord added, "No branch can bear fruit by itself; it must remain in the vine. Neither can you bear fruit unless you remain in Me" (John 15:4).

The principle of "remaining" in Christ and He in the disciple is hard to fathom, but the illustration of the branch and the vine is hard to misunderstand. In the same way that the branch maintains contact with the vine and draws its life from it, so the disciple must, at all costs, maintain contact with the Master and draw life from Him. In the immediate circumstances under which Jesus taught these truths, the contact was physical; but He had already been alerting the disciples to the tremendous possibilities of a spiritual relationship with Him, through the Holy Spirit, which would surpass even the most intimate physical relationship they had known with Him. The Twelve were quite skeptical about this. In fact, when He told them that the new relationship with the Spirit would be to their advantage, they were confused. It is not hard to see why!

It would take some time before they could possibly realize that it is one thing to have the Master striding along beside you and quite another to have the risen Lord living, through His Spirit, within you. But as He taught them about the vine and branches, He was clearly alluding to this aspect of their faith, which, as yet, was completely foreign to them.

The disciples were to take all necessary steps to ensure that no estrangement should come between them and their indwelling Master. Perhaps He was helping them to better understand this requirement when He talked to them about being His friends. It is hard for some people to visualize how to maintain a relationship with an invisible Lord, but when the relationship is painted in terms of friendship, it comes remarkably closer to home. If you want to maintain a friendship, you aim to please. You look for ways to express how you feel and you do it in practical ways. The way to show our appreciation to Christ is to "obey." He explained, "You are My friends if you do what I command" (15:14). Nothing is more pleasing to Him than to see His disciples doing what He wants them to do.

There are different ways of obeying! Some people are like military men, who obey because they have no other option. Others are like children, who obey because they know the odds are so stacked against them that they will be in trouble if they don't! Still others are like employees, who calculate that it is to their advantage to obey because, if they don't, they will be fired, demoted, or put on a shelf. None of these "obediences" is what the Master had in mind. Instead, Jesus was thinking of the kind of obedience that comes when a person who—recognizing the privilege of being a friend of someone far superior to him in every way, and wishing to express appreciation for this status which he never deserved—joyfully and exuberantly does everything his friend desires, and thoroughly enjoys doing it.

Remaining in this relationship is not the act of a moment. It is the attitude of a lifetime. It involves ongoing growth and constant application. The Master said: "If you remain in Me and My words remain in you, ask whatever you wish, and it will be given you" (15:7). Christ's emphasis on the Word and prayer now becomes unmistakable. We need to be continually in tune with His words and constantly in touch with His Father to know what He desires and to draw from Him the power to do it.

Suppose a disciple becomes negligent in reading the words of Christ. The result will be a deterioration of spirit, in the same way that there is a deterioration of muscle and sinew if protein is left out of the diet. What's more, the malevolent influences of the believer's enemies will infiltrate his life, in much the same way that toxic fumes can infiltrate a sleeping body. The loss of energy and the pollution of body may not be immediately apparent; but given time, and not very much of it, the effects will be plain to see.

I have often been amazed at the naïveté of some men and women who have talked to me about their marital problems and the proposed solutions. But not any longer, because I have found that many people know more about the soap operas than about Christ's words. When they confront a situation similar to the one being portrayed on the screen, they automatically relate to what they are watching and almost instinctively react in the way the actors react. The fact that the secular solution is far removed from the biblical solution is of little concern, because either they don't know what Scripture says on the subject or they have so much toxicity in their spiritual bloodstream that their thinking and decision-making are no longer responsible.

If this sounds far-fetched, let me assure you that even those who find themselves in positions of mature Christian leadership have fallen morally, not because they were suddenly overwhelmed by an impossible temptation, but because they had allowed biblical truth to be swamped by worldly error, which they had been slowly but surely imbibing. Such people often respond to their misdemeanors by talking more about psychology than sin and more about personal fulfillment than individual responsibility.

Going back to John's gospel, note that the study and application of Scripture is integrally linked to the practice and enjoyment of prayer. The Master made a wonderfully sweeping promise: "Ask whatever you wish, and it will be given you" (15:7). Taken out of context, this could make a superb rationale for all kinds of irresponsible praying. He had also, however, just said, "You may ask Me anything *in My name*, and I will do it" (14:14, italics added). To ask in His name is to ask as His representative, in the same way that to act in His name means to act on His behalf. Therefore, the validity of the thing asked for can usually be ascertained by asking such questions as, "Would Christ want me to do or have that? Is this something Jesus would be interested in?"

When children are young, it is not unusual for their mom to ask them to run next door to the neighbor's to borrow some sugar. The neighbors know that is a perfectly normal request and hand over the sugar. But if the same kids go to the bank and ask the teller to give them $10,000 on their father's behalf, they would immediately be put on inquiry.

When disciples relish their friendship with the Master, study His Word and apply it in their lives, and then ask Him for legitimate things necessary to fulfill His stated objectives, the relationship is sweet and the results are manifest. Fruit grows all over the place. That brings us to another aspect of fruit-growing in the disciple's life. Increased productivity is what the Father has in mind! If the Master is the Vine, the disciples are the branches, and Christlike character is the fruit, then the Father is the Gardener who tends the branches with a view to producing more and better fruit. And how does He do this? By the uncomfortable but definitely necessary expedient of pruning. The Master told the disciples, "He cuts off every branch in Me that bears no fruit, while every branch that does bear fruit He trims clean so that it will be even more fruitful" (John 15:2).

In the same way that a vine left to itself will produce all kinds of shoots that serve only to drain the energy of the stock, so discipleship, if left unattended and unaccountable, will degenerate into an energy-sapped, nonproductive exercise. In the same way that the old vine of Israel, described by Jeremiah, slipped back into wildness, the disciple's life has "wild" tendencies which must constantly be held in check. The Father is committed to seeing that this task is done; and He does it by instituting certain disciplines such as prayer and the study of His Word, which we have already mentioned. In addition, He places disciples in relationships where they are accountable to those who care for their spiritual well-being—this is, of course, one of the functions of the local church as well as a responsibility of concerned friends. Recall a couple of examples with me:

After the Lord's ascension, Peter became a leader of the church in Jerusalem, where he was called upon to discipline Ananias and Sapphira for their lies against the Holy Spirit. Not only did the guilty pair die, but the whole church, warned of the seriousness of their offense, was challenged to a degree of commitment which they had not previously known. We are told, not surprisingly, by Luke, "Great fear seized the whole church and all who heard about these events" (Acts 5:11). Peter himself was not exempt from a little pruning either. In his case, it was Paul who was called upon to confront him with an unwelcome exposé of his hypocrisy. Nor was Paul immune. We are never told what his "thorn in the flesh" was, but we do know that it was given to him by God "to keep [him] from becoming conceited" (2 Cor. 12:7).

It is therefore appropriate for us to recognize that divine structures, loving people, or circumstances can be utilized by the Father in the pruning process. In the case of Ananias and Sapphira, the pruning produced a deeper reverence for the things of God; in Peter, a cutting away of immature inconsistencies; and in Paul, a stripping away of a native arrogance to which he could easily have fallen prey.

It goes without saying (but I'll say it anyway!) that pruning is painful, and, accordingly, is often resisted. It is not uncommon for disciples who are being disciplined by their churches for some inappropriate behavior simply to pack their bags and go to another church. I knew a man who was being disciplined, quite rightly, who not only left his church but founded another! When this happens, the necessary pruning does not take place and the result is more wild growth and less real fruit. On the other hand, where the pruning, however painful, is realized as being necessary and ultimately helpful, the results can be most beneficial to all concerned.

My dad often used to comment that "the same sun that melts wax hardens clay." In the same way, discipline from the Lord produces in some people a sweetness and a maturity; but in others, bitterness and regression. The reason is simply that those who accept the pruning, produce; and those who reject it grow sour grapes that set everyone's teeth on edge.

Besides pruning the fruit-bearing branches to make them more fruitful, God the Gardener also "cuts off every branch . . . that bears no fruit" (John 15:2). These branches, Jesus tells us, "are picked up, thrown into the fire, and burned" (v. 6). So not only is there living wood that needs to be pruned, but there is deadwood that needs to be removed altogether. It is serious when living branches grow wild and they become considerably less productive than they are intended to be. But it is much more serious when deadwood clutters the vine. Unpruned wood fails to produce its potential; deadwood has a vast potential for destruction, decay, and disease—and usually produces it!

Perhaps Judas Iscariot was the most striking example of deadwood associated with a living Vine. He had just departed from the group at the time the Master taught about the pruning process (John 13:30); and the disciples assumed that, because Judas was the treasurer, he was going to attend to some financial business. It was some hours before they understood the significance of his betrayal and subsequent actions; but when they did, they realized that they had been living with a dead branch without even knowing it.

Modern disciples need to be aware that the community of believers is always vulnerable to deadwood taking over. This is a state of affairs which, far from producing the character and activity of the living Master, produces those things which militate against Him and His cause. Unfortunately, many of us have heard of churches "dying on the vine," but we may not always have known why. Either the real branches became unfruitful through an unwillingness to respond to the Gardener's pruning, or the church itself became a collection of people who failed to recognize that vital union with the living Christ is the *sine qua non* of spiritual experience.

Shortly after I had resigned my position in the bank at the age of twenty-nine, in order to embark on a career of full-time ministry, I was stricken with a throat ailment so painful that public speaking was impossible and normal conversation difficult. I was devastated by this turn of events, because there was some doubt if I would be able to resume preaching. I had never been ill in my entire life, so I had no experience of suffering—and it showed in my attitude! The thing that particularly bothered me was that, having given up a secular career in order to devote myself to preaching, it now looked as if I might be unable to do either.

During the time of enforced inactivity, however, I felt that I had to address the fundamental question, "Did I love preaching about the Lord more than the Lord about whom I preached?" It didn't take long for me to discover that the thought of being a preacher and traveling around the world had been most attractive to me, and may well have been a major factor in my decision to leave the bank—even though I would have denied such a suggestion vigorously. But the pruning process was at work, and in the end I reluctantly admitted what was going on in my own heart, reaffirmed my genuine desire to serve the Master wherever and however He wished, and agreed that if He didn't want me to preach ever again I would be happy to go on loving Him. At that time in my life I was a disciple of Jesus Christ very thinly disguised as a sidelined preacher. ◆

Failure Isn't Final

LITTLE DID THE DISCIPLES realize that they had unwittingly become the very focal point of an epic, cosmic struggle. The Master suddenly announced, "Simon, Simon, Satan has asked to sift you as wheat. But I have prayed for you, Simon, that your faith may not fail. And when you have turned back, strengthen your brothers" (Luke 22:31). The very fact that the Master reverted to the old name "Simon" must have surprised Peter, and presumably it was done with a view to reminding him that he was still a work in process. But the news that Satan had actually been seeking permission to wreck Christ's tiny group of followers must have overshadowed any other surprise he may have experienced.

Peter's response, however, suggests that while he understood things may have been getting out of hand, he had no real idea of what lie ahead for Jesus or the Twelve. "Lord, I am ready to go with You to prison and death," he boasted. But the Master knew better, saying, "Before the rooster crows today, you will deny three times that you know Me" (vv. 33-34).

It is not hard to explain what happened to Peter in terms of a self-sufficient man learning his own inadequacy the hard way. But there is much more to it than that. Peter and his companions were the targets of a satanic attack and their sole defense was the Master's commitment to pray for them.

Down in the trenches these men were going to be fighting against a hostile crowd and their own inner tendencies to save their own skins. But in the High Command the struggle was much greater. It was the Prince of Darkness versus the Prince of Peace. The former was committed to undoing all that the Father had planned for the redemption of the world; the Father, on the other hand, was committed to seeing His Son, the Master, accomplish against all odds that for which He had become incarnate. Peter could have had practically no idea that he was caught up in this momentous combat.

While the disciples could do little to assist the Master in His impending work of redemption through the cruel death on the cross, their involvement would become absolutely crucial once the cross and its resultant resurrection had been safely accomplished. Therefore, it was profoundly important to Satan that they should be stopped; and it was even more important to the Master that they survive the onslaught. We should not overlook the fact that Jesus, knowing all this, still granted permission for His men to be put to the test. He was well aware that they would go through deep waters and that they would all forsake Him. But if they were going to be His men—fitted for that to which they had been called and had gladly volunteered—they must go through their baptism of fire. But not alone! He was praying for them.

I must admit that I spend a lot of my time in the trenches, fighting the daily battles of life in general and ministry in particular, without any conscious recognition of the cosmic nature of the struggle in which I, a modern-day disciple, am involved. In a sense, this is not all bad, because if I were to always concentrate on that ultimate aspect of the battle, I might forget that I am a foot soldier, not the Supreme Commander. On the other hand, if I were to always overlook the titanic aspects of the struggle, I could easily become blasé as a disciple and purely professional as a minister. My life as a disciple would then be lived in terms of my ability and energy rather than through obedience to the Master and dependence on His all-sufficient grace; and I would be using the "tools of my trade" instead of true spiritual weapons, without which there is no victory against a foe of Satan's stature.

With a final word about His life's work "reaching its fulfillment" (Luke 22:37) and a cursory acknowledgment to His
worried disciples that two swords were enough protection,
Jesus led the way to the Garden of Gethsemane. The disciples
by this time were physically and emotionally drained, and
when the Lord asked them to pray with Him, they were unable to keep their eyes open. He was disappointed, but understood their weakness, and returned to the solitary vigil of
unspeakable tension and importance. Shrinking from the
thought of being made a sin offering Himself, recognizing
what being estranged from the Father would entail, and brac-
ing Himself for the outpouring of divine indignation on a lost
world's sin, He prayed for the last time that if at all possible
another way of redemption might be found. But to no avail.

Sadly, the disciples were asleep on the job while the Saviour anguished alone. Indeed, even the best disciples still fall
asleep on the job, and sometimes at the very moment that
they most need to be alert. This knowledge serves to remind
us all that there is still a long way to journey on the road
called "following."

Things deteriorated rapidly from that point. Judas arrived
leading a heavily armed group which included the high
priests and their guards. As Iscariot identified the Master and
soldiers moved to arrest Him, Peter stood in the way, swing-
ing vigorously with a sword which caught Malcus, the slave
of the high priest, on the side of his head and chopped off an
ear. Jesus had to sternly remind Peter that violence was not
necessary; then healing the wounded man's ear, He allowed
Himself to be led away.

The phrase "Peter followed at a distance" (Luke 22:54) can
be regarded purely as a piece of narrative detail, or it can be
seen as indicative of Peter's condition at that moment. Peter
had made a commitment to follow, but the sheer tension of
following had gotten to him. He couldn't pull out—he had
made a promise! But he couldn't keep up—he was scared! So
he followed at a distance. Close enough to maintain contact,
but far enough removed to avoid association. Near enough to
technically fulfill a promise, but far enough away to escape
the consequences if at all possible. Apparently the rest of the

disciples, with the probable exception of John, fled the scene. Peter's performance, though less than spectacular, was way above average. For the moment.

But worse was yet to come. As Peter watched the proceedings with mingled horror, disbelief, and shame, he was confronted by no less than three separate people on three separate occasions, all of whom questioned him about his relationship with the Master. The disciple denied three times that he even knew Him. Evidently the Master, knowing what was transpiring across the courtyard, looked in Peter's direction at that critical moment. He said nothing. Nothing needed to be said. He had already told Peter that Satan was after him and that he would deny knowing Him before dawn. And He had been right. Peter's boastful insistence that he would follow through right to the very end was proven hollow and empty. The proud, rugged Galilean broke down and cried like a baby.

But why was he crying? He had believed that the Master was Messiah—that He had come to restore the glory of the former days—and he had thrown himself wholeheartedly into His campaign. Now his dreams were shattered. I have seen political campaign workers, having spent three years of their lives working all hours for their candidate, only to see him lose the nomination, burst into tears before the television cameras. Perhaps Peter felt like them. Or maybe it was a case of a proud man seeing for the first time his own limitations and being horrified at what he had discovered. He had never backed down from anybody in his life—not even the Master. But when push came to shove, he couldn't handle an impertinent young servant girl who was about to blow his cover. Afraid of neither man nor beast, Peter was not so much afraid of a young woman as he was afraid that he might have been exposed to something with which he could not cope.

Whatever combination of factors contributed to Peter's dismay, I suspect that it was the look of the Master which broke him up the most. What that look said we can only surmise; but knowing the Master, it certainly was not, "I told you so." No, it was probably a look of intense pain and hurt, tinged with love and compassion. The pain and the hurt came from

Christ's own sense of deprivation; He was now left without any human advocate, however distant. The love and compassion reflected what had always been there—a tremendous affection for this big, bumbling man who deep in his heart wanted to be his best for God, but who deep in heart wasn't able. Just like the rest of us. When the Master looked lovingly at Peter, He was looking at a typical man who reflected the hideous consequences of the Fall—the event which had turned the pinnacle of divine Creation, man (male and female), into a shambles, and robbed us of our ability to be what we in our noblest moments longed to be. And in that look was reflected the love for fallen mankind which brought Jesus from the heights of glory to this moment, in order to restore us to our rightful position of fellowship with Creator and Saviour.

They say Helen's face "launched a thousand ships," but the Master's look can break a million hearts, because it shows something that mankind has never seen anywhere else—pure unadulterated love for failing, feeble humanity. Disciples who are following at a distance are in deep danger of denying their allegiance to the Master; they need to remember the look which first drew them to Him and then steadfastly return it.

There are many things over which Scripture draws a discreet veil. The failure of spiritual people is certainly not one of them. And Peter is not the only one whose failure is described in detail. But Scripture does not catalog the sins of saints in order to encourage casual indifference to disciplined discipleship, even though some people may be happy to use this information as a rationale for unwarranted behavior.

A man came up to me after the morning service one Sunday while I was preaching through Genesis and said, "Boy, I just love listening to you preach."

"What is it that you enjoy?" I asked.

"I love it when you talk about these guys like Abraham and Jacob and all the others."

"And what is it you like about them?"

"They're such an encouragement because every one of them is worse than me!" he responded with a grin—to my chagrin!

I had to spend a little time assuring this gentleman that that was not the point of the exercise. Perhaps all of us tend to look at the Peters of the church and take comfort in their failures, and so settle down to similar performances. But this is an abuse of the Word. Surely Scripture is explicit about the failure of early believers only to remind us of our own vulnerability, and to encourage us to learn from the mistakes that they made.

While the Lord went to His personal Calvary, Peter went through his own deep agony. Afraid for his life, ashamed of his failure, aghast at what had happened to the Master, he was utterly adrift in a sea of confusion. Broken dreams, broken promises, broken heart. After all the excitement and promise of the last three years, there was nothing to look forward to but the daily grind of eking out a living on the lake. Dark was his tunnel and, as yet, there was no light at the end of it.

Fortunately, some of the women were made of sterner stuff than the men and they had stayed around the cross long enough to know that the Master's body had been removed and buried in Joseph of Arimathea's tomb. Not satisfied with the burial Jesus had received, they prepared spices and perfumes, rested on the Sabbath, then the following day set out to care for His body. They were worried about the heavy stone at the tomb's entrance, but when they arrived they were amazed to discover it had been rolled away, and even more incredulous to see that the body had disappeared. Slowly the truth dawned on them. He had risen from the dead, just as He said He would!

Rushing back to the disciples, who must have been a sorry sight by this time, the women told them what they had seen and heard. "Nonsense," they scoffed. But Peter went to see for himself; rushing to the tomb, he looked in and "saw the strips of linen lying by themselves, and he went away, wondering to himself what had happened" (Luke 24:12). The women had already made the connection between what had happened and what the Master had predicted. But not Peter! Not yet!

People react differently to their circumstances. Some, like the women at the tomb, are very adept at putting two and two together, arriving at four, and proceeding with their lives. Others have a harder time making things fit. Some people find it much more difficult than others to admit that they have been terribly wrong. This could have been the case for Peter. Or perhaps he was thinking to himself, "If He really is risen, then I will have to face Him. And what can I possibly say to Him about my denial and desertion?" Maybe half of him hoped it was true and the other half dreaded the thought.

Peter was not left wondering too long. On that same day, the Master appeared to him personally and returned in the evening when the disciples were together. To say that they were dumbstruck is to put it mildly. To suggest that they were not embarrassed is to fail to recognize the momentous nature of the preceding days' events. Yet the Master spent no time upbraiding them for their failure; instead, He addressed what, to Him, was more significant—their lack of faith. To Him, it was perfectly clear that He would rise again. He had told the disciples repeatedly that He would. They were amazed that He had. He would only have been amazed if He hadn't! They still found it hard to believe. He found it hard to believe that they found it hard to believe!

Despite the resurrection appearances, much was still to be done. There was no easy road back for these wounded men, but the Master had time. In fact, He appeared to be in no hurry at all. That's the good news for all those injured disciples who have gone through Satan's sifter with less than flying colors. The Lord understands the tremendous odds we face, and, while the hurt and disappointment that we fail remains, His love and care prevail, leading to His gracious ministry of restoration in our lives.

A particularly close friend of mine had been a foreign missionary for a number of years. Unfortunately, she had run into some problems on the field, and eventually felt she could not carry on. She was deeply distressed about the way she had been treated, but more distressed that she felt she had failed the Lord, her mission, and her supporting church. As we talked, I realized that one of the main problems she faced was not knowing what to say to the people in the church. Fortunately, we are a large congregation, so I told her to communicate the bare minimum of information to those people who really needed to know what happened; and then to sit on the very back row of pews, soak up the love of her close friends, saturate herself in the Word, and give herself time to heal. This she proceeded to do, and in a matter of a few months she not only regained all her former spiritual vitality but went on to become a most effective minister in ways which she had never previously suspected she was able.

Like my friend, many disciples of Jesus Christ have failed under Satan's sifting and need the chance to recover. Let us uphold these wounded warriors and be the Lord's instruments of healing. ◆

Gone Fishing

PETER, WONDERING AS HE WANDERED, was trying hard to get his mind together. What was he to make of this strange turn of events? What exactly had happened to the Master and why? What was he going to do with his life? Did the Master still figure in his plans? Or more accurately, did Peter still figure in the Master's plans? In fact, did the Master have any plans anymore? Peter needed space. He may also have needed some money, so he decided to do what he knew best. "I'm going fishing," he declared.

Despite his monumental failure, Peter apparently was still held in high regard by the other disciples, for they promptly decided to follow his example. They piled into the boat, headed out at sunset, toiled all night, and caught nothing at all. As the sun was rising over the low-lying hills, they headed for shore.

At this point someone standing on the beach called out to ask whether they had caught anything. He called them "children" or "lads," which must have seemed rather strange. But they were in no mood for niceties, so they simply shouted back, "No."

"Throw your net on the right side of the boat and you will find some," yelled the stranger. Surprisingly they did, and more surprisingly, they came up with a bumper catch—153 big ones to be exact!

Immediately, John, true to form, said, "It is the Lord." Peter, equally true to form, threw on his jacket, jumped overboard, and headed for land. What Peter was thinking or whether he was thinking, we have no way of knowing, but that he acted with his accustomed impetuosity is clear to see. When he got closer to shore, he noticed a charcoal fire like the one beside which he had warmed himself when he denied the Lord. With his emotions frazzled, and given the extreme sensitivity of the subject, I have no doubt that the sight of that fire brought everything flooding back into his memory.

Disciples of long standing have never been exempt from frazzled emotions and confused feelings. They were never promised a rose garden in the first place and, that being the case, they have frequently found themselves in situations which have produced more questions than answers. But in the midst of the confusion, one question is paramount. And it is not asked *by* the disciple; it is presented *to* the disciple. This question was now posed to Peter.

"Simon son of John, do you truly love Me more than these?" (John 21:15) The address was formal, but the voice was warm. And there was no doubting the identity of the speaker. That voice was too familiar to allow for any more doubt. It was the Lord and He was asking the disciple the most important question of all. Peter promptly answered in the affirmative, emphasizing the "You," as if to say, "You are asking me? You of all people know what's going on inside me."

"Feed My lambs," Jesus instructed.

Again Christ asked the same question; again Peter repeated the answer; again the Lord gave the same instructions. Then strangely, the conversation was repeated once more. Wait a minute! Three times Peter had been asked about his relationship to the Master and three times he had denied any knowledge of Him. Three questions, three denials. Now three questions and three affirmations. The fire in the courtyard. The fire on the shore. This could surely not be coincidence!

Satan had desired to sift this man like wheat and leave nothing but chaff. But the Master was not about to allow the Evil One free rein. True, the disciple must be allowed to go through the testing, but not alone. True, he must find out what he was made of, but not in such a way that he would never survive the discovery. Now he was being given every chance to reflect on his true feelings toward the Master while vividly conscious of the events which had brought those feelings into question.

A closer look at the dialogue, however, shows that there was much more to it than simple repetition. For example, Jesus and Peter used different words for *love*. In His first two questions, the Master used the word *agape*, but Peter replied with *phileo*. But in His third question, the Master used *phileo* and Peter stuck with the same word. *Agape* is the stronger word, *phileo* the weaker; and while it may be unwise to make too much distinction between the two, neither can we ignore the usage nor the distinctives involved. It would seem reasonable to conclude that Peter was affirming his love for the Master, but not at the depth the Master was asking. This in itself indicated something of the struggle Peter was enduring. It reminds me of the old hymn:

> Lord, it is my chief complaint,
> That my love is weak and faint,
> But I love Thee, and adore,
> O, for grace to love Thee more.

Love goes through stages. It grows through experiences. It matures with time and deepens with opportunity. Peter's love for the Lord had been severely threatened because it had collided head-on with his innate love for himself. It was only when Peter looked into the depths of his own despair that he realized his misery was a commentary on his love for Christ. Because of this, he was able each time to answer the Lord's question unequivocally, promptly, and realistically.

When the Master abandoned the higher word for love and used the one with which Peter was more comfortable, He was in essence saying, "That's fine, Peter. I understand. I know you love Me and that's all I want to know. But I want to hear you say it so that you can hear it too, and can have the benefit of knowing what I already know." For the Master, knowing all things, knew what lay hidden in the bottom of Peter's heart. He needed to give Peter a chance to dig it out for himself, look at it, and rejoice again in a love that had survived—battered and bruised, but intact.

The situation was not too dissimilar to that which we encounter all too often in pastoral counseling. A happily married man is attracted to another woman and, instead of recognizing the danger signals, allows himself to drift along with his feelings until he becomes unfaithful to his wife and unfair to the other woman. The affair is subsequently discovered and the awful recriminations begin. Fortunately, the man admits his sin, turns from it, and seeks his wife's forgiveness. She, although hurt and disappointed, freely extends it to him. It is only when he is safely back in the care of his family that he realizes how much he really does love them. The sifting he went through should have been resisted, but it wasn't. If he had followed the path of righteousness, he would have saved everyone considerable pain; but he didn't. The one bright spot, however, is that he has learned through the sad experience how deeply his love runs. He would have learned the same lesson by saying no to the temptation in the first place.

Back to the questioning on the shore. The Master specifically asked Peter, "Do you truly love Me *more than these*?" Unfortunately, we have no way of knowing exactly what He meant by *these*. Did He mean, "Do you love me more than these other disciples love Me?" At first sight, that might seem like a counterproductive question in light of the competitive spirit which had prevailed among the disciples. On the other hand, since Peter had regularly bragged about his superior commitment to the Lord, it might have been a perfectly reasonable question designed to make him reevaluate his claims.

Or perhaps Jesus meant by His question, "Do you love Me more than you love these other men?" While Peter's devotion to the Lord had been shown suspect, his devotion to the disciples was apparently intact. In fact, as we have seen, it appears that he still commanded their respect and may well have been functioning as their leader. So this interpretation is not without merit.

Another possibility is that the question Jesus asked—in the

context of the lake and the boats and the fish—was accompanied by a gesture which embraced them all. Then the question would be, "Do you love Me more than all these things and people that legitimately make up your everyday life?" Whatever we decide about the exact meaning, there is no doubt that the Lord's question was one which demanded Peter to prioritize his love.

This kind of question is so hard to answer in the abstract. It's rather like asking a young man whether he loves his life more than his country. In peacetime he may not be able to answer the question because he is not even sure what the question means. But if the enemy attacks his homeland and the tanks are rolling up the streets of his neighborhood and the shells are wrecking his home, he can answer the question very quickly. If he heads for the bushes and keeps his head down, his answer is obvious. If, on the other hand, he promptly volunteers to serve in some capacity, whether combatant or noncombatant, his answer will be equally obvious.

Many people have talked to me about their love for the Master as it relates to other issues of life. My advice to them is not to worry about answering the question until it needs to be addressed in concrete situations. For instance, the girl who never had a date may ask herself whether she loves the Lord more than the guy who sits next to her in class. The question is important but possibly unanswerable—unless and until this guy asks her to enter into a relationship with him that would violate her professed loyalties to the Master. In the same way, the businessman sitting at his mahogany desk may ponder whether he loves his business more than he loves the Master. The question may be academic until he is faced with an opportunity which involves some shady dealings. If he goes ahead with the shady business while rationalizing that he can build the church a new sanctuary with the profits, he may find the answer to his question, and discover that it is not the one he expected.

Conversely, the interrogation to which the Master subjected Peter had a specific objective. He was not interested in making Peter squirm; He wanted to get him on track again. Hence the three instructions which followed the three ques-

tions and answers. Here again, they are not just repetitive. The instructions, recorded in John 21:15-17, were these:
Feed My lambs.
Shepherd My sheep.
Feed My sheep.
You don't feed lambs the way you feed sheep. You only feed a lamb if it loses its mother. Then it is necessary to take the frail little animal under your arm, put a bottle of warm milk to its mouth, and let it suck away. But you don't do that to a big smelly sheep. You put it in a pasture, provide protection for it, and let it do its thing. In much the same way, Peter was being commissioned to take the truth of Christ to those who were neophytes and needed feeding like lambs, but also to nurture those who were more mature by showing them how they could feed themselves and draw nourishment from the truth. In other words, this meant Peter would need to develop great insight into the human condition, great understanding of human need, and considerable flexibility in addressing different people in different situations.

But shepherds do more than feed. They also lead. It is true that in the Western context, shepherds spend a lot of time chasing sheep either with dogs or on horseback or tractors. But this is a foreign concept to Eastern shepherds and would have no place in the Master's intentions. As the psalmist rejoiced that the Good Shepherd "leads me beside the quiet waters" (Ps. 23:2), so Peter and his fellow disciples were to lead God's people, by example and teaching, into the way of truth and righteousness.

Disciples of the Master do not and cannot love Him in a vacuum. To love Him is to love what He loves; and that includes the Father, the Father's cause, and the Father's creation. That is why the question about loving Him must in some way be linked to the statement about serving Him. Remember Jesus stipulated that it was *His* sheep who needed caring for! That Peter got the message is abundantly clear from his own writings. He wrote specifically to those who were "scattered" (1 Peter 1:1). He talked about them desiring "pure spiritual milk" (2:2). And he addressed them as those who "were like sheep going astray" but who had subsequently "returned to the Shepherd" (2:25).

One of my greatest joys is spending time with the young pastors who serve with me on our church staff, and the group of elders who oversee the fellowship. They differ widely in ecclesiastical backgrounds, theological training, spiritual gifting, ministerial priorities, senses of humor, and style of dress. But they have two things in common. Every one of them is distinguished by a love for the Lord and a desire to serve the people. They are, without exception, disciples of Jesus Christ skillfully disguised as shepherds of God's flock.

◆

But What About Him?

RECENTLY I TALKED to a man whose wife had been unfaithful to him. He was understandably distraught, but he was not concerned only about the breakdown of his marriage. He told me that he had prayed that the Lord would intervene—and He hadn't. At first, this caused him to question the Lord's love for him; but as time went on, he had begun to question whether the Lord even existed. His case is not atypical. But it is serious. When spiritual discouragement sets in, disciples are particularly vulnerable.

Immediately after Jesus had given Peter the benefit of His total attention and had outlined for him the ministry of shepherding to which he was now called, the Master added, "When you were younger you dressed yourself and went where you wanted; but when you are old you will stretch out your hands, and someone else will dress you and lead you where you don't want to go" (John 21:18). [For our benefit John comments that the Master was predicting the God-glorifying manner in which Peter would eventually die. Tradition confirms that Peter was subsequently crucified and that he personally requested to be executed upside down.]

Then Christ dropped the clincher: "Keep on following Me." Evidently the Master was gently forewarning Peter that when the going gets particularly tough, the disciple needs to be particularly conscious of following one step at a time.

The problem for all of us is that difficult circumstances may demand so much of our attention that inadequate attention is given to the nurturing of our devotional life at the very time when added attention is necessary. The moment we need to be particularly aware of the Lord's grace in our lives, in order to cope with a significant problem, is the same moment we tend to so concentrate on the problem that the grace is overlooked.

In my pastoral ministry I have often observed that disciples who find themselves under the gun will often become slack in their worship attendance. This, sadly, is the very time that they should be aware of the added necessity of being among the Master's people, concentrating on the things of the Master, and sensing His presence in a special way through the warmth of fellowship, the giving of thanks, and the ministry of the Word. This was specifically the case with the man whose wife had been unfaithful to him and whose faith had consequently taken a nosedive. We all need to be aware that, though we will not likely suffer the same type of death Peter suffered, the appropriate response is to "keep on following" when the heat is on.

But there was another problem for Peter. No sooner had he digested the unwelcome prophecy of his impending demise than he noticed "the disciple whom Jesus loved" walking behind them. "Lord, what about him?" asked Peter with typical candor (John 21:21). Being told that you are going to have a difficult time is hard to bear, but such is human frailty that it helps if you know everyone else is going to have a similar experience. Peter wanted some assurance that if he was going to be required to walk a rocky course, he would at least have some company! No such luck!

Christ answered, "If I want him to remain alive until I return, what is that to you? You must follow Me" (v. 22). Or to put it bluntly, "Mind your own business!" But notice also the renewed command, "Follow Me!" If there is one thing a disciple needs to learn, relearn, and re-relearn, it is the absolute necessity for ongoing following. In Peter's experience, we have seen him follow tentatively at first. Then enthusiastically and impetuously, even to the point of running ahead, turning around, and blocking the path! Later we see him following at a distance, and then not even following at all. Eventually we see him pick up where he left off, sadder and a little wiser. But even so, the Master finds it necessary to remind him more than once, "Keep on following."

There is a sense in which the most effective discipleship takes place in a group. Note that the Master discipled His followers en masse rather than one-on-one. The Apostle Paul reminded Timothy to adopt a similar procedure: "The things you have heard me say *in the presence of many witnesses* entrust to reliable men who will also be qualified to teach others" (2 Tim. 2:2, italics added). In both these cases, one of the obvious advantages (apart from productivity!) was the interaction of group members, which in and of itself would be a great learning experience. For example, the tensions among the Twelve about who would be the greatest must have taught them as much about themselves and their own failings as any other part of their training.

But there is also an inherent problem in group discipling: it can produce unhealthy, competitive, and comparative following—the kind of situation where we are so busy watching how the other person is getting on that we forget that we are supposed to be following the Master.

Young divorced women have told me on more than one occasion how difficult it is for them to meet with married women their own age, because they feel so resentful of the other women's marriages. Instead of being able to share together in the fellowship of believers, they have found themselves being consumed by bitterness. "Why should I be saddled with a failed marriage and literally left holding the baby, struggling to make ends meet without anyone to care if I live or die, while she has everything so easy?" they wonder. Ultimately, these women have to be encouraged to recognize that their discipleship must be lived out in less than ideal circumstances. Other women may indeed have it easier, but they all are disciples who have to follow the same Master. The circumstances are secondary.

Gladys Aylward was a tiny, fiery missionary whose work with children in China during the Japanese occupation was memorialized in the film *The Small Woman.* One day as she read in her Bible that the Lord would supply her needs, she told Him, "I need a husband. You promised to supply my needs, so I expect You to send me a husband." I remember hearing her tell the story with such effect that, as she came to this part, she paused, looked around the room, and added, "And he never came."

She went on, "Somewhere in this world is a man to whom God said, 'Go to China and marry Gladys Aylward. And he never came!'"

I must admit at this point that one of my colleagues, a single man about Gladys' age, was sitting near me in the meeting. I pointed to him and whispered, "Was it you?" He denied it vehemently!

I smiled and turned my attention back to Miss Aylward in time to hear her say, "So I said to God, 'God, why don't You do something about this man, whoever he is and wherever he is?' And God leaned out of heaven and said, 'Gladys Aylward, mind your own business!'"

I remember thinking, "I didn't know God leaned out of heaven, but I *do* know He requires me to mind my own business."

It is interesting to note that Peter apparently learned this particular lesson well, because he later wrote, "If you suffer it should not be as a murderer or thief or any other kind of criminal, or even as a meddler" (1 Peter 4:15). The Greek word translated *meddler* is *allotriepiskopos*, meaning "someone who oversees (or keeps an eye on) someone else's affairs."

The reminder to follow the Master irrespective of what others are doing is particularly relevant to those who seek to serve the Master, but feel that their efforts in no way compare with those of others and, therefore, are worthless.

On numerous occasions I have been invited to speak at conferences for pastors and their spouses. I have noticed that it is usual to invite pastors of large churches to address such gatherings, but it is also normal for most of the attendees to come from relatively small churches. This has made me nervous because I sense that some of the pastors from smaller churches, after hearing about the "success stories" of larger churches, may be tempted to try and achieve similar results in their own situations. This may prove impossible, and the result is that the small-church pastor feels even more discouraged. His frame of mind can become, "What have I done to deserve a situation like this? Why can't I be part of a growing, bustling, successful church instead of serving year after year at the First Church of Podunk? And what's so great about their pastor anyway? I remember him in seminary. He couldn't parse a verb to save his life. Come to think of it, neither could I!" The Lord's answer is the same: "Mind your own business. Follow Me!"

Jesus went on to tell Peter that He was perfectly free to keep the beloved disciple alive until the Second Coming. He was exaggerating only to make a point, but unfortunately the misinterpretation was "shared" (probably as a prayer request!), and then repeated until "the rumor spread among the brothers that this disciple would not die" (John 21:23). It is sad that this sort of thing happened even among the original disciples, but it is also instructive. At least it shows that the disciples, even at the end of their three-year crash course, still had a long way to go. They were into rumors and gossip and meddling in each other's affairs just like we are in the contemporary church. But what can be done about it? The answer is simply: "When the rumors are flying around, make sure that you don't repeat anything until you are sure it is true. Then make sure it is helpful and necessary."

At a recent staff meeting, one of our young pastors asked for some advice in answering a problem that had been presented to him. Apparently a member of our church had visited another area church and, in the foyer at the end of the service, was approached by two couples who asked why she still attended Elmbrook since we were "planning to abolish baptism!" I advised my colleague to tell the worried person that the Christian church had been practicing baptism in excess of 1,900 years, and therefore it was unlikely that we would be successful in any attempt to abolish it even if we wanted to—which we most certainly did not. We then turned to the more serious matter of reminding ourselves of the importance of being so committed to following the Master that we will not be eager to compete, compare, or criticize.

I learned a lot about this kind of thing from my father. He was a gifted speaker who traveled a rather limited area to minister at various churches and youth groups. When I was still new in the pulpit I was given the opportunity to travel much further afield than he, mainly due to the different area of the country where I was living. On one occasion I went home to see my parents, and my dad asked me to speak at a local youth rally. I was surprised to be invited because no one in the area knew I was coming home. But he told me that someone in the group had found out, and asked him if he would mind stepping aside. He had gladly agreed to do this, but I was perturbed that they would be so thoughtless as to request such a thing. He not only insisted that I speak, but came along to listen!

As we talked about my message on the way home, Dad shared specific ways in which he had found it helpful and asked me questions about the application in his own life. Little did I realize at that time that this would be the last conversation I would have with my father, for he died of a heart attack a few days later.

The memory of the conversation is understandably precious, but the attitude of my dad is what sticks in my mind almost thirty years later. He could have asked the Lord, "Why does this kid of mine get opportunities I never get? I've been faithful over many years and he's only just starting. Why would they want him rather than me?" He asked none of these things because he didn't even think them. He was too busy following the Master himself and rejoicing that the Master had put me to work too. We need more like him! He was a disciple of Jesus Christ skillfully disguised as my dad. ♦

Disciples Make Disciples
Make Disciples Make Disciples

THE MASTER TOLD the disciples to meet Him on a certain mountain in Galilee. They dutifully arrived in the right place at the right time and the Master Himself appeared. By this time they had become a little more accustomed to meeting somebody who had recently risen from the dead, but there must have been some degree of puzzlement on their part as they gathered. Matthew tells us, "When they saw Him, they worshipped Him; but some doubted" (Matt. 28:17).

The "some" who did the doubting are not identified, and this has led some commentators to suggest that other people in addition to the Eleven were in attendance. On the other hand, as no mention is made of any others, some insist that several of the Eleven were still in a state of ambivalence. The key words *worship* and *doubt* indicate, they say, that some were ready to prostrate themselves before the Master in adoring availability, while others were markedly hesitant.

Without in any way trying to settle the question of who attended the meeting, I would have to say that in my own experience there have been times when I have been adoringly available and others when I have been decidedly hesitant. So I would have no difficulty believing that the Eleven were not unanimous in their response to the Master.

It is interesting to remember that we read a lot about some of the Eleven after the Ascension and not a word about the others. Does this mean that some of them settled down into an uninvolved passivity that carefully ignored the Master's final instructions? I have no way of knowing, but I do know that there is no shortage of disciples today who are in the hesitant category when it comes to a serious response to the Lord's final instructions.

Two of the most common reasons for uninvolvement in any endeavor are feelings of inadequacy and insecurity. The Master addressed both of these concerns. He told the disciples, "All authority in heaven and on earth has been given to Me" (Matt. 28:18). It is relatively easy to believe that Christ has authority in heaven, but from a purely practical point of view it is the understanding and conviction that He has authority on earth that helps reluctant disciples to deal with their feelings of inadequacy. There is great encouragement for even the most inadequate disciples in the knowledge that they are not standing on their own feet, but in His sandals when they truly proclaim the truth in the power of His Spirit.

The Heaven and Hell Club was a particularly unpleasant place where the teenage prostitutes and drug users of a northern England town hung out. The club had two stories—the upper, where the lights were switched on, called "Heaven"; and the lower, where darkness prevailed, called "Hell." The establishment was presided over by a tough character known to all as "Grotty Bob." He ruled the place by the force of his personality and the power of his fists; nobody messed with Grotty Bob.

One night the Heaven and Hell Club burned down. As it not-so-coincidentally had happened, a number of my friends and I had opened a Christian club next door. For rather obvious reasons it was called the Catacombs, as it was situated in the cellars under a bombed-out office block. The night after the fire, Grotty Bob came into the Catacombs and asked where the boss was. Everybody looked at me and I tried to look like a mural.

Marching over to me, he demanded, "Bring out your bouncer." (For the sake of those of you who had a sheltered childhood and never visited a youth club in northern England, a bouncer is a tough guy who maintains control by the simple expedient of bouncing people down the stairs and out of the club if they arouse his displeasure.) As he made his demand, I noted he was placing brass knuckles on his fists, and I knew that he intended to fight our bouncer for control of our club.

"I can't bring him out right now, Bob," I replied in a voice that refused to stay in a manly octave.

" 'Course you can bring him out," he shouted. "Get him out here! I don't have all night!"

"Bob, I can't bring him out."

"He's chicken. That's why you won't bring him out."

"He's not chicken. He's just not available."

"Well, what's his name? I'll find him," he bellowed, becoming more belligerent by the minute.

"Our bouncer's name is the Lord Jesus Christ," I heard myself saying.

The most remarkable thing happened. At the name of the Lord Jesus, the color drained from Bob's face, his knees lost their strength, and he sank into a chair looking stunned. (I must have looked equally stunned!) The fight went out of him and he listened like a small child as I told him about what we were trying to do for the kids of the city in Christ's name and with His authority. I cautioned Bob against doing anything to those who represented the Lord, because if he did, he might find himself up against Someone he couldn't handle. Bob nodded quietly, got up from the chair, and walked slowly from the club. I wish I could tell you that he was converted to Christ that night and is now the Archbishop of Canterbury, but I'm afraid I know nothing more about him, for I never saw him again. But that night the Catacombs were alive with the sheer vivacity that comes from knowing that inadequate people are made adequate when they draw on the authority of Jesus Christ—which is as relevant on earth as it is in heaven.

Another of the Master's statements is no doubt more understandable to us now than it was to the Eleven when He made it. He told them, "And surely I will be with you always, to the very end of the age" (Matt. 28:20). The disciples were still trying to fathom the significance of the Resurrection without, as yet, paying much attention to His promised exodus and what would follow. With the benefit of 20/20 hindsight, we know that Jesus was referring to the remarkable infilling of the Holy Spirit in the lives of His disciples, so that at any given moment, under any given set of circumstances, they could be assured of His immediate and dynamic presence in them, in order that He might work through them. In this truth they were to discover the sense of security which they, and all who followed in their footsteps, needed so desperately.

I have always been surrounded by friends and colleagues who fortunately have a sense of humor. So when, more than twenty years ago, I received a letter inviting me to attend the "Polish Millennium," I ignored it and wondered which of my crazy friends had gone to the trouble to produce a letter which purported to come from Poland. Imagine my surprise when some weeks later I got a telephone call asking why I had not responded to the invitation. I explained that I thought it was a practical joke and was told, "It's no joke. We're about to celebrate the thousandth anniversary of Christianity in Poland and we want you to come and speak to our pastors."

"That's great. I'd love to come. But why me?" I asked.

"Well, the Catholics wanted the Pope, but the Communists wouldn't let him come. And the Free churches wanted Billy Graham, but the Catholics blocked that. So we thought since nobody knew who you were, we could get you in all right!"

"Sorry I asked," I replied!

So one cold winter's day I flew into Warsaw. No one was at the airport to meet me. I had no contact names or addresses. While other passengers collected their bags and left, I stood and waited. And waited.

After what seemed an eternity, I was startled by a voice behind me. "Briscoe?"

I whirled around and saw to my dismay a man wearing a long coat with the collar turned up and a hat pulled down over his eyes. My mind immediately filled with statements like, "It wasn't me. I haven't done anything. I'll come quietly, but I must see a lawyer." I didn't realize how nervous and insecure I could be until that moment. But I need not have worried, for a great grin spread across his face between the collar and the hat, and to my astonishment he hugged me and kissed me three times! Then, grabbing my bag, he hurried me out of the airport and onto a trolley bus where, as we hung onto the straps in the crowded aisle, he proceeded to talk to me in a loud voice about the Lord Jesus. I noticed people were listening and he said, "Oh, many of them speak English, so speak up loudly. Your ministry in Poland has begun." I suddenly began to feel very much at home with this man. The reason was simple. He was with me and he knew what he was doing!

This was the sort of thing the Master was trying to impress on His disciples then and wants us to understand now. "Surely I am with you" spells security in any language. Armed with this sense of adequacy and security, the Eleven were to embark on the mission for which they had been prepared, perhaps unwittingly, over the last three years.

And exactly what was this mission? Jesus commanded, "Go and make disciples of all nations, baptizing them in the name of the Father and of the Son and of the Holy Spirit, and teaching them to obey everything I have commanded you" (Matt. 28:20). By now these men had a good working knowledge of what discipleship meant and had enough material to begin teaching. Granted, they were still in the learning-and-following process and would be till the day they died; but that did not mean they should be reluctant to teach what they knew.

The scope of Christ's mandate was immense. The disciples were to go and make disciples of all nations. They were Jews and had engaged in a ministry which the Master reminded them was primarily aimed at the "lost sheep of Israel." This was not to be construed as disinterest in the Gentiles on the Master's part, but rather as a matter of priority. Nobody needed to remind Jesus that the Father's grand plan was that through Abraham *all* the nations of the earth would be blessed. Now the time had come for the nucleus He had trained to launch out into the mind-boggling task of reaching a world with the Gospel, multiplying themselves again and again and again.

Three things would be required of the disciples: namely,

"going," "baptizing," and "teaching." It would be impossible
to win the nations if those called to do the winning didn't
visit the nations. The truth of this is as incontrovertible as it
is inconvenient. It means in simplest terms that disciples have
always needed to examine their own understanding of the
Master's call in order to see if He wants them to make the
necessary sacrifices involved in reaching out to disciple other
ethnic groups.

The "going" for a considerable number of Christians will
entail crossing an ocean, but for those who honestly believe
that this is not what the Master wants for them, the command
is no less crucial. How about traveling across town to another
ethnic group in the same city, or across the street to a neighbor family, or even across the office to a colleague? There is
always somewhere to go, and that means crossing some kind
of barrier—whether geographical, political, sociological, or
just plain psychological. It should be apparent to all disciples
in any era that the discipling of the nations does not happen
when the disciples who know don't go.

The "baptizing" part of the Lord's commission should not
be overlooked either. Unfortunately, much debate and disagreement about baptism have occurred down through the
centuries, and this has somewhat obscured the issue. It is
interesting to me that the Didache, a summary of Christian
teaching from the second century, states, "Baptize ... in living water. But if you have not living water, baptize in other
water; and if thou canst not in cold, in warm. If you have
neither, pour water thrice on the head." How's that for admi-
rable flexibility!

It does not require any great genius to recognize that modern practices of baptism have strayed a good bit from the
early days. This may be because we have lost sight of the fact
that for first-generation Christians, baptism was a major
break with their society and a definitive statement about their
identification with the Master. Whatever mode of baptism we
prefer today, we should be careful not to lose sight of the
significance of baptism as a break and an identification. In a
Christianized culture this is sometimes difficult, but as the
lines between the secularism of our modern societies and the

stand of committed disciples become more clearly drawn, the true meaning of baptism may once again become more apparent.

Some years ago, I visited a Muslim nation where I had the great privilege of spending time with several delightful old men who had embraced Christ as Saviour. One of them was the brother of a prominent mullah, or teacher, and he had been told that as long as he kept his faith to himself, the family would leave him alone. But if he chose to be baptized, he would be brought before the authorities and beaten with heavy bamboo rods in the public square after prayers on the Muslim sabbath. Shortly after I visited them, these men decided they would go ahead with their baptisms, despite the threats to their health and possibly even their lives. It was this kind of baptism, the stand-up-and-be-counted type, that the Master commissioned.

While it may be difficult to reproduce such clear-cut, take-it-on-the-chin commitment in a baptismal ceremony today (and it may not be necessary to try), there can be no doubt that the disciples we are called to make are those who will publicly confess (in much more than a purely ceremonial context) that to which they privately adhere. This must be a major part of our discipling objective.

Over the course of three years the disciples of Jesus had gone through a wonderful learning experience. They had sat at the Master's feet and walked at His side. They had watched Him in action from the fifty yard line, as it were; asked Him questions; argued His points; and emulated in many instances His example. Having first come to Him, they then learned to love Him, trust Him, and obey Him. Now it was their turn to teach what they had learned.

This was to be no purely academic exercise, because the net result of the lessons was to be obedience. "Teaching them to obey *everything* I have commanded you" was and still is an inclusive instruction. Not just the attractive parts and certainly not just the easy sections. Everything! And the clear implication here is that the lessons would only truly be learned when the behavior of the learner was changed. The disciples were to be in the business of seeing lives transformed through obedience to the authoritative Word of God, made possible through the power of the indwelling Spirit.

Any disciple who has struggled with learning and obeying has no difficulty recognizing that disciple-making is not a task for wimps. It is not easy to be obedient when we don't want to obey. Why then should we expect those we are trying to lead to obedience to get excited about having to make some big changes? Will they not resist? Won't they have all kinds of excuses? Is it possible they may be as devious as we have been ourselves? Might we run the risk of losing their affection when we stand firm on the Word of God despite their protests?

Even during the last few days while I have been trying to complete this manuscript it has been necessary for me to leave the word processor more than once and spend time with several disciples who are struggling with some of the things the Master commanded. One of them does not like what Christ said about marriage and not letting man put asunder what God has joined. Another didn't want to go and speak to a sister whom she had offended because it would be embarrassing. But the Master said disciples should do that sort of thing. Yet another was having to face the unpleasant fact that his business ethics were in danger of falling short of disciple standards. Of course, even though I have been on the disciple trail for many years, during the same few days I have been reminded by some of my friends on the trail that my attitudes were not what they might have been, and my expectations of some of my colleagues had been unreasonable. I was astonished to hear these things, but I needed to be told so I could make the necessary adjustments and corrections. Indeed, these last few days have been like the rest of them— spent in teaching-learning, in discipling and being discipled.

The methodology of teaching has been up for grabs for some time, but even a cursory study of the way the original disciples were taught shows numerous techniques the Master used, including: example, illustration, lecture, experience, opportunity, encouragement, and rebuke. So I see no reason for the debate. Surely He showed us plenty of ways to teach and learn; and I sense that if we can invent some new ones, He won't mind, as long as they're biblically sound and we finish up with more disciples.

Perpetual motion is a wonderful idea! No one, unfortunately, has been able to invent a device which would achieve it. The problem is how to start something in motion which then would be capable of producing its own energy, thus sustaining the motion for an indefinite period. But while earthly inventors continue to search for a solution, I believe there is already a spiritual dynamic set in motion by the Master which has this same potential. It's the "disciples make disciples make disciples" principle. All it requires is for disciples to continue learning and following, and at the same time to be in a relationship with others which allows them the opportunity to teach what they are learning or have learned. In the less than immortal, but highly memorable words of Augustus De Morgan:

> Great fleas have little fleas upon their backs to bite 'em
> And little fleas have lesser fleas, and so on, *ad infinitum.*

It's the *"ad infinitum"* idea of disciples making disciples which so intrigues me and which causes me to challenge you now. Take a good, hard look at your own learning-following-imitating discipleship. Then ask yourself who the people are around you whose lives are being so impacted by you that they too are about to begin, have just begun, or are faithfully following the discipleship road. If you can't readily answer this question to your own satisfaction, then why not make this a matter of major spiritual concern and take whatever steps may be necessary to rectify it. Because there is no doubt about it—when the principle works, it is close to perpetual motion; but when some individual misses an assignment, the system is severely affected and the job the Master bequeathed to us does not get done.   ♦